PUBLIC ADMINISTRATION

PUBLIC MANAGEMENT AND CHANGE SERIES

Beryl A. Radin, *Series Editor*

Editorial Board

Titles in the Series

PUBLIC ADMINISTRATION

Traditions of Inquiry and Philosophies of Knowledge

NORMA M. RICCUCCI

Georgetown University Press / Washington, D.C.

Library of Congress Cataloging-in-Publication Data

Riccucci, Norma.
   Public administration : traditions of inquiry and philosophies of knowledge /
   Norma M. Riccucci.
      p.   cm.— (Public management and change series)
   Includes bibliographical references and index.
   ISBN 978-1-58901-704-7 (pbk. : alk. paper)
   1. Public administration.   I. Title.
JF1351.R4648   2010
351—dc22
                                              2010001636

♾ This book is printed on acid-free paper meeting the requirements of the American National Standard for Permanence in Paper for Printed Library Materials.

15 14 13 12 11 10   9 8 7 6 5 4 3 2

Printed in the United States of America

In memory of my beloved parents,
Tosca and Giorgio Riccucci

CONTENTS

ILLUSTRATIONS

ACKNOWLEDGMENTS

The ideas and research presented in this book emerge from my own intellectual grappling with the logic of inquiry and philosophy of science in public administration over the past few decades. The hope is that it will pave the way for further debate and investigation into this critical area within the field and, perhaps more broadly, the social sciences.

I am grateful to a number of persons who helped along the way. Beryl Radin has provided an extraordinary level of support, encouragement, and guidance, and I am particularly indebted to her. Others have engaged in constructive deliberations and conversations or have provided useful feedback in the writing of the book, including David H. Rosenbloom, Howard E. McCurdy, Craig W. Thomas, Kaifeng Yang, Gregg Van Ryzin, Gerald Miller, and the anonymous external reviewers. I also wish to thank my dean, Marc Holzer, for his support as I wrote this book during my sabbatical leave. Finally, I am grateful to Don Jacobs for his leadership and direction in the culmination of this project.

Introduction

To doubt everything or to believe everything are two equally convenient solutions; both dispense with the necessity of reflection.

—JULES HENRI POINCARÉ, *La Science et l'Hypothèse*
(Science and Hypothesis)

The field of public administration today supports and promotes a variety of research traditions. Some are wholly quantitative, whereas others are qualitative. And some are mixed, relying on both qualitative and quantitative methods. In addition, some research is empirically based, whereas other studies are strictly normative. In fact the various journals of public administration and its subfields are bound to or characterized by these research traditions. For example, one of the leading journals in the field, *Public Administration Review* (*PAR*), publishes articles ranging from postmodern critiques (e.g., Spicer 2007) to the testing of hypotheses in regression models (e.g., Bretschneider 1990). Other journals, such as the *Journal of Public Administration Research and Theory* (*JPART*), more recently have published articles relying on complex quantitative techniques and analyses. *Administrative Theory & Praxis* (*ATP*), conversely, publishes normative and theoretical dialogues on public administration. In addition, some journals are geared toward both practitioner and academic audiences (e.g., *PAR*), whereas others are pitched exclusively to academics (e.g., *JPART* and *ATP*). All this research, notwithstanding the methodological approach taken, adds value to the field's literature and theoretical base. One journal is not superior to the other; nor is one research approach more desirable than another. And because of its disciplinary basis (i.e., applied) and related history, as will be seen in this book, public administration will always support a range of different research traditions.

To be sure, there continues to be conflict and dissonance among scholars as well as practitioners over the relevancy and applicability of the various research or epistemic approaches. On the one hand, there is a pragmatic desire to derive knowledge from common experience; on the other, there is the impulse to appear scientific. Even the lingering concerns over the "identity" of the field, particularly whether it is an "art" or a "science," are masked by questions such as "What are the appropriate methods for studying or theory building in public administration?" The public administration community continues to ask, for example, whether public administration should strive to be a science, and thus predisposed to the "tools" of science, including its analytic methods.

In the mid–twentieth century Dwight Waldo and Herbert Simon fomented a debate regarding this conundrum over the logic of inquiry in public administration. As is discussed in this book, it created tensions and sometimes ill will among both researchers and practitioners. The question of whether public administration is an art or science, whether it is driven by values or facts, will never be satisfactorily answered, because of the lack of a consensus among the community of scholars within the field. Their debates have raised questions about the philosophical and methodological underpinnings of public administration that continue to challenge the field even today.

In fact, during the past few decades, several studies have examined the quality of research methodology in public administration (e.g., McCurdy and Cleary 1984; Perry and Kraemer 1986; Stallings and Ferris 1988; Houston and Delevan 1990; Box 1992). With the exception of Box's essay, these studies, based on evaluations of dissertations and journal articles, have found that research in public administration lacks analytical rigor in accordance with the norms and practices of the social sciences. These studies have also concluded that research in public administration focuses on issues pertaining to the practice of the field to the exclusion of theory building. Similar to Box, this book challenges the narrow conception of science and analytical rigor assumed by these studies, and it illustrates the broad range of research traditions that add value to both the field's theory and practice.

Thus rather than staking a claim for any particular set of research tools, this book enters the debate from the standpoint of reason: It seeks to provide a critical review of theory-building research and public administration epistemology so as to demonstrate that there is a diversity of traditions to studying and conducting research in the field, ranging from interpretive to postmodern critiques. Topics or issues in public administration can be based in, for example, empiricism or rationalism, and studied inductively or deductively, qualitatively or quantitatively, or both. The intended purpose of this book is to engage reasonable-minded public administrationists in a dialogue on the importance of heterogeneity in epistemic traditions, and in general to deepen the field's understanding and acceptance of its epistemological scope. The field would be more consonant with the recognition that knowledge is derived from impressions on both the intellect and the senses.

SCOPE OF BOOK

Chapter 1 sets out the framework of the book by examining the debates over ontology, epistemology, and methodology in the field of public administration. Somewhat contiguously, ontology asks "What is reality?" and "What is existence?" It questions whether reality can be an objective phenomenon or if it is a social, political, or gendered construct. Epistemology asks "What can we know?" and "How do we know what we know?" Depending upon the ontological framework, it seeks to define the relationship between the research and the researcher (i.e., whether researchers are detached from the research or inextricably linked to it). Methodology asks "How should efforts to know be executed?" It asks whether researchers should seek reality and truth via the manipulation of data, through the mind, or through the words expressed, for example, in texts and behaviors. These debates are tied to the intellectual development of the field. For example, the highly acclaimed debate between Dwight Waldo (1948) and Herbert Simon (1946) over the role and limitations of science in public administration is addressed. This debate, in turn, served as a catalyst for shifts in the field toward, for example, behaviorism. Although these themes have been addressed previously in the public administration literature, chapter 1 represents my foray into the debate and sets the stage for subsequent chapters.

For instance, questions of whether public administration is an art or a science, whether it is based on fact or value, are derivatives of the Waldo–Simon debates and effect epistemic approaches and theory building in the field. A related question is whether public administration has a paradigm. These two closely related perspectives on the logic of inquiry, which frame the essence of this book, are addressed in chapter 2.

Chapter 2 argues that public administration lacks a paradigmatic base because of the very nature of the field, which is applied, and thus characterized by experience and practice. Moreover, those practices and the institutions that control and drive them are imbued with politics, which further precludes the field from acquiring a paradigm. The chapter further shows that because the field lacks a paradigm, it cannot be treated as a normal science in the Kuhnian sense (Kuhn 1962). Instead, public administration is a postnormal science, one that is driven by multiple norms and traditions, and hence can be studied through a variety of epistemic and ontological lenses.

Chapter 3 illustrates how public administration is not alone in this self-consciousness quagmire. Other disciplines in the social sciences also struggle with whether they are governed by a paradigm and with similar types of ontological, epistemological, and methodological quandaries. The scientific developments in the field of public administration are thus contrasted with the scientific approaches in related fields such as political science and policy analysis. Chapter 3 presents a host of examples and hence may be useful to social scientists in other disciplines as they study similar issues concerning the scope, theory, and methods of their fields.

Chapter 4 presents a typology for epistemic traditions in public administration. More specifically, it provides a framework for a number of research approaches: interpretivism, rationalism, empiricism, logical positivism, postpositivism, and postmodernism. The different ontologies and epistemologies associated with these approaches point to appropriate methodologies and recording techniques for each. Again, the purpose is to show the range of heterogeneity in research traditions for public administration.

Parenthetically, some may argue against the use of the term "logical positivism" or "positivism" in favor of, for example, the "scientific knowledge" approach. However, because this book challenges the traditional use of the term "scientific," logical positivism is the designated term. Moreover, although some may claim that positivism or logical positivism as a movement is dead, its legacy in the field of public administration as a philosophy of science perdures. As Frederickson and Smith (2003, 110) recognize, "Positivism and the canons of social science methodology and epistemology tend to dominate academic perspectives toward management theory in public administration."

Chapters 5 and 6 provide examples of different epistemic traditions in public administration research. Qualitative approaches are addressed in chapter 5, and quantitative ones are covered in chapter 6. For instance, interpretive studies in public administration relying on content analysis are qualitatively based and illustrated in chapter 5. Examples of postmodernist critiques as well as qualitative empiricism are also presented in chapter 5. Research approaches growing out of the behavioral movement are steeped in logical positivism; examples of this type of quantitative research are identified in chapter 6. As the chapters indicate, both qualitative and quantitative research have contributed greatly to theory building in public administration.

Chapter 7 provides examples of research in mixed methods, which combines qualitative and quantitative methods. The benefit of mixed methods—or triangulation, as it is often called—is that it draws on the strengths of both qualitative and quantitative techniques. Moreover, a mixed-methods approach is particularly suitable for applied fields in that it fosters better understandings of complex social phenomena.

Chapter 8 serves as a summary, providing a synopsis of epistemic traditions in public administration. It also emphasizes a caveat regarding this undertaking: Some may be so hardened in their views about the logic of inquiry in public administration that they will remain intolerant of any form of epistemic heterogeneity. This book is not for the faint of heart.

Intellectual Heritage and Theoretical Developments

IS PUBLIC ADMINISTRATION AN ART OR A SCIENCE?

It is necessary to deny . . . that empiricism is the essence of science.

—Dwight Waldo, *The Administrative State*

The conclusions reached by a particular school of modern philosophy—logical positivism—will be accepted as a starting point.

—Herbert A. Simon, *Administrative Behavior*

There are innumerable accounts of the historical developments in the field of public administration (see Frederickson and Smith 2003; Stillman 1999).[1] Every introductory textbook in public administration chronicles the various periods or stages of development in the field (e.g., the orthodox or classical period; the administrative behavior movement), especially from the standpoint of practice. Indeed, the field of public administration emanates from practice, or the practical activity of administration and management in the public sector. In the United States, Woodrow Wilson is generally credited with a shift in focus toward "The Study of Public Administration" as is further discussed below.

By all accounts there tends to be a consensus in the field that there is no single or central core theory of public administration but that it can instead be characterized by its rich intellectual heritage (see, e.g., Rosenbloom 1983b). In effect there is a fundamental lack of agreement regarding the scope of public administration. Some have argued that this dissonance has led to an identity or intellectual crisis in the field (e.g., Ostrom 2008).[2] But public administration is not unique here, and indeed, this has not diminished the stature of our applied field. As will be addressed in this book, other branches of the social sciences are afflicted by this same multiple-personality syndrome. For example, sociology has been beleaguered by conflicting theoretical perspectives, which have clouded its intellectual boundaries as a field (see Collins 1986). Moreover, the dissention among sociologists about their identity as a field is "exacerbated by the philosophical and methodological controversies about the feasibility and quality of social scientific research" (Crane and Small 1992, 199). Thus, other social science disciplines face quandaries similar to that of public administration.

The lack of a core theory has had implications for both the practice and study of public administration.[3] In particular, it has led to a multitude of approaches to or theories about how public administrators (practitioners) ought to administrate and how public administrationists (scholars) ought to study public administration or engage in theory building and testing.[4] For example, in his seminal piece "The Study of Public Administration," Woodrow Wilson in 1887 endeavored to prescribe that in order to promote efficiency, public administrators should not engage in the enterprise of politics. Thus was born his famous (infamous?) politics/administration dichotomy, which continues to be addressed, ad nauseam, in public administrative teachings today.

Other broad frameworks of public administration called for different administrative action or behavior. For example, the human relations school pointed to the importance of human behavior and in particular the interactions between workers and management. Motivational and psychological theories, as opposed to economic ones, were deemed critical for studying and understanding the behavior of people in organizations (see, e.g., Follett 1924; Metcalf and Urwick 1942).

Wilson's single piece of scholarship, which received virtually no attention in its day, is ascribed to the advent of public administration as a "discipline" or educational endeavor—what Waldo (1980) later called the "self-conscious" study of public administration.[5] However, it is important that Wilson's discourse was clearly set in the context of practice, not study. It endorsed rational, instrumental behavior and was followed by a series of writings from others advancing the same prescriptions for administrative behavior, or the practice of public administration, which were cumulatively labeled "classical" or "orthodox" theory. Considered among the most notable are the deliberations of Frederick Taylor (1911) and his call for scientific management, a doctrine supporting a reliance on "science" for determining the best way of performing jobs and then ensuring, for the sake of efficiency, that the jobs are performed according to that "one best way."

The works of Gulick and Urwick (1937) were also praised at the time for generating a "science" of administration, whereby adherence to a set of prescribed principles, better known as the "principles of administration," would promote efficiency in government, much like scientific management or Taylorism would for private industry (see, e.g., Stivers 2000). These and other orthodox theorists contributed conceptual themes to the earliest period of our field's intellectual or theoretical development.[6] And the continual calls for "science" revolved around the practice of public administration, not the study.

It was in yet another iteration of the field's intellectual development that a challenge was lodged against the so-called scientific underpinnings of the practice of public administration and, concomitantly, offered prescriptions for the *study* of public administration. Herbert Simon's (1947) groundbreaking *Administrative Behavior*, along with his earlier writings (e.g., Simon 1946), debunked the principles of administration and argued that a science of public administration could never be built upon a foundation of *practice*, as Taylor, Gulick, and others had advocated. For one thing, Simon challenged the classic textbook accounts of administrators' ability to make rational, economic, utility-maximizing decisions. Instead, he makes it clear that the "capacity of the human mind for formulating and solving complex problems is very small compared with the size of the problems whose solution is required for objectively rational behavior in the real world" (Simon 1957, 198). Administrators, according to Simon, make decisions that "satisfice," that is, are both satisfactory and sufficient for the situation at hand. In effect, Simon replaced the maximizing goal of choice with that of satisficing.

Simon also argued that public administration could and *should* be studied from the viewpoint of scientific principles as they were rigorously applied in other social sciences. Thus the administrative behavior movement in public administration and its principal architect, Simon, paved the way not solely for progress in the study and theory building of public administration but also for polemics.[7] Simon fomented a debate about the appropriateness of certain epistemic traditions or approaches to study and theory building that continues to mire the field even today, influencing the development—or, more appropriately, the conceptualization—of other intellectual undertakings in the field (e.g., policy analysis and public management, which are addressed in chapter 3). But could a field built on pragmatism be studied from the standpoint of "science," as traditionally defined in the social sciences?

This was a question asked by another major figure in public administration, Dwight Waldo, who took exception to many of Simon's claims about "scientific" inquiry into public administration (also see Dahl 1947). The following section examines their ongoing exchange over epistemology, ontology, and methodology, which frame the core thesis of this book—that there is no one best way to study public administration.

THE WALDO–SIMON DEBATE

Herbert Simon's *Administrative Behavior*, first published in 1947, marked the beginning of a critical new movement or direction in the field of public administration, particularly from the standpoint of study or theory. As a direct attack against the orthodox theorists, Simon offered, among other concepts, a fact/value dichotomy. Many interpreted his conceptualization of a fact/value dichotomy as a direct analogue to the politics/administration dichotomy advanced by Wilson. And many, including Waldo, viewed Simon's classification as a call for the adoption of scientific "principles" that could be used for the *study* of public administration.

Simon (1997, 48) argued that when studying organizations and administrative behavior, "what is needed is empirical research and experimentation to determine the relative desirability of alternative administrative arrangements. The methodological framework for this research is already at hand in the principle of efficiency. If an administrative organization whose activities are susceptible to objective evaluation can be studied, then the actual change in accomplishment that results from modifying administrative arrangements in these organizations can be observed and analyzed."

The acquisition of knowledge about public administration, according to Simon, should be based in *fact*: empirically derived, measured, and verified. Values, he claimed, had no place in the study of public administrative phenomena. He urged scholars to take as their primary unit of analysis the decisions that administrators made. Decisions could be studied scientifically in terms of their effects as well as the processes for making them. Such inquiry, in his view, could be value free and morally neutral, uncorrupted by the normative preferences of the people involved.

Simon (1997, 48) called for the necessity of objectivity and that "sufficient experimental control be exercised to make possible the isolation of the particular effect under study from other disturbing factors that might be operating on the organization at the same time." He went on to say that administrative studies heretofore have been devoid of experimentation and have not observed "fundamental conditions of methodology." As he stated: "In the field of public administration, research has been carried out without the benefit of control or objective measurements of results . . . [and thus] have had to depend for their recommendations and conclusions upon *a priori* reasoning" (Simon 1997, 49).

Parenthetically, Simon recognized that the administrators involved in decision making would not behave in this manner. The activities of practitioners, he and James March recognized, were circumscribed by "boundaries of rationality" (March and Simon 1958, 171). Due to human limitations, decision makers in government did not maximize their preferences or find optimal solutions, but rather they satisficed.[8] In practice, they made decisions that met minimum standards of satisfaction, sufficient for the task at hand. Thus Simon expected persons engaged in the *study* of public administration to behave rationally and scientifically, but not the people toward whom those studies were directed.

Simon was heavily influenced by the behavioral revolution beginning to sweep the social sciences. This revolution found its historical roots in the philosophical movement known first as positivism, as advanced by Auguste Comte, and later as logical positivism, as advanced by the Vienna Circle.[9] Rudolph Carnap, of whom Simon was an acolyte, was a major proponent of the logical positivist movement. Carnap (1996) called for "The Elimination of Metaphysics Through Logical Analysis of Language." Through his work and that of a number of others, particularly Simon's, logical positivism in public administration became synonymous with *quantitatively* empirically based research traditions, subject to verifiability or validity. As noted, Simon opined that public administration should be based in fact: empiricism, measurement, verification. This and related issues will receive greater attention in chapter 4.

In sum, whereas leaders of the early public administration movement sought to discover principles of administration founded in practice, Simon and his followers championed research about administration based on scientific principles.

Dwight Waldo emerged as one of Simon's chief critics. In *The Administrative State*, Waldo (1948, 1984) sought to understand why the scientific perspective had played such a large role in early efforts to understand the administrative state.[10] Waldo recognized that from Luther Gulick's efforts to classify administrative studies as a social science to Frederick Taylor's promotion of "scientific management," scholars in the newly emerging field had embraced the philosophy of scientific inquiry (also see Waldo 1968 and, more generally, Charlesworth 1968). Waldo (1984, 177–78) observed that empiricism and experimentalism "have a prominent place in the methods of physical science." However, he strongly argued, "there is much in scientific method which is nonempirical and nonexperimental." Why then had administrative scholars so enthusiastically adopted the language of science? As was typical for his work as a whole, Waldo saw the phenomenon in cultural terms. Administrative studies, he observed, were distinctly pragmatic, often drawing knowledge from common experience. Yet administrative scholars wanted people to respect that experience. What better way, Waldo (1984, 168–69) suggested, than to mask pragmatism in "the prestige of the 'philosophy of science'"?[11]

Waldo maintained that Simon and his followers unjustifiably sought "to place large segments of social life—or even the whole of it—upon a scientific basis" (Waldo 1984, 57). Waldo (1984, 171) elaborated that although some administrative matters may lend themselves to "treatment in the mode of natural science, . . . administration is generally suffused with questions of value." He stated that "a physical science problem is a problem of 'What is the case?' An administrative problem is characteristically a problem of 'What should be done?' Administrative study, as any 'social science,' is concerned primarily with *human beings*, a type of being characterized by *thinking* and *valuing*" (Waldo 1984, 171, emphasis in the original).[12] For him, many of the most important issues affecting the development of the administrative state were simply not amenable to the methods advanced or supported by logical positivism (see Dubnick 1999).

An explicit, explosive tête-à-tête erupted between Waldo and Simon in 1952 in a series of antagonistic, vitriolic commentaries published in the *American Political Science Review*.[13] It centered on a few issues but, most prominently, on philosophies of science from the standpoint of ontology, epistemology, and, by inference, methodology.[14] The debate often devolved into ad hominem invective and antipathies.

Waldo, a political theorist, not surprisingly stakes an ontological claim on public administration as democratic theory. He states: "If administration is indeed 'the core of modern government,' then a theory of democracy in the twentieth century must embrace administration" (Waldo 1952a, 81). He makes a case for democracy as the core value of public administration, a sort of triumph of democracy over efficiency, the latter having consumed the classical or orthodox theorists in the first half of the twentieth century. He methodically critiques classical theories of public administration and goes on to say that "Herbert Simon's recent *Administrative Behavior* presents a closely reasoned defense of the notion of an abstract science of administration centered on efficiency" (Waldo 1952a, 87–88). He then presents a forceful argument that the principal obstacle to the further development of a democratic theory of public administration is the belief that "efficiency is a value-neutral concept" and that the field must accept "efficiency as the central concept in our 'science'" (Waldo 1952a, 97).

In a coup de grâce Waldo (1952a, 97) goes on to say that "to maintain that efficiency is value-neutral and to propose at the same time that it be used as the central concept in a 'science' of administration is to commit one's self to nihilism, so long as the prescription is actually followed." Waldo's (1952a, 97) footnote to this statement reads: "I believe that there is no realm of 'factual decisions' from which values are excluded. To decide is to choose between alternatives; to choose between alternatives is to introduce values. Herbert Simon has patently made outstanding contributions to administrative study. These contributions have been made, however, when he has worked free of the methodology he has asserted."

Simon responded to Waldo's assertions with his own blend of sarcasm and diatribe. He begins by stating: "I am impelled to do this in part because the faults of Waldo's analysis are characteristic of the writings of those who call themselves 'political theorists' and who are ever ready to raise the battle cry against positivism and empiricism" (Simon 1952, 494). He goes on to say:

> Study of logic and empirical science has impressed on me the extreme care that must be exercised, in the search for truth, to avoid logical booby traps. For this reason the kind of prose I encounter in writings on political theory, decorated with assertion, invective, and metaphor, sometimes strikes me as esthetically pleasing, but seldom as convincing. Since I am unable to discover definitions in Mr. Waldo's paper for his key terms, since he does not set forth his basic premises in any systematic fashion, and since his propositions appear to skip from philosophy to psychology to history and back, I have not succeeded in reconstructing the syllogisms by which I presume he reached his conclusions. (Simon 1952, 494).

In a final blow, Simon takes aim at Waldo's philosophy of science in the broader context of an attack on political theorists and their contributions to public administration. Simon (1952, 496) argues: "Quite apart from whether Mr. Waldo's premises are right or wrong, I do not see how we can progress in political philosophy if we continue to think and write in the loose, literary, metaphorical style that he and most other political theorists adopt. The standard of unrigor that is tolerated in political theory would not receive a passing grade in the elementary course in logic, Aristotelian or symbolic."

Waldo (1952b, 501) gets the proverbial last word with this mordant admission:

> According to my philosopher friends who regard themselves as empiricists, logical positivism has performed a useful function as an apparatus of criticism; but we have already reached a point from which it can be viewed in perspective, not as the end of philosophy, not as The Philosophy, not even as the Philosophy of Science, but merely as another chapter in the history of philosophy. Presently, three "generations" contest for leadership of a movement that is seriously divided. May I state for the record, though I had hoped that I had made it clear, that I am not opposed to positivism and empiricism as whole bodies of thought or techniques of investigation or action. I am indebted to self-labelled positivists and empiricists for much information, clarification, and stimulation.

It is interesting to note that in "The Administrative State Revisited," a retrospective examination of Waldo's treatise, that appeared in a 1965 issue of *Public Administration Review*, Waldo softened his criticism somewhat. He had been "bludgeoned," he said, by Simon in the early 1950s, causing him to examine more closely the central tenets underlying the philosophy of logical positivism. Upon closer examination, Waldo recognized that there was a tendency for many, including himself, to view public administration as "*normative* theory, i.e., theory about how organizations *should* be constructed." A more contemporaneous treatment, he confessed, would recognize the possibility of an administrative theory that was "nonnormative" (Waldo 1965, 13; emphasis in the original).

Waldo concluded that although he found the philosophy of logical positivism to be "acute and useful" in some ways, it was "limited and misleading in others." He went on to say that "Logical Positivism is content to take one area of human experience and treat it as the whole" (Waldo 1965, 13 n. 14). In the end, he recognized that public administration might benefit from a combination of different methodologies.

Parenthetically, the Waldo–Simon debate was followed by other deliberations that underscored the question of how to appropriately study public administration. For example, the new public administration (NPA) was a conscious effort to neutralize the effects of the behavioral revolution spurred by Simon. The NPA was a movement that grew out of the Minnowbrook Conference, where a group of scholars led by Dwight Waldo gathered in 1968 to study the relevance of public administration to social problems of the day such as the civil rights movement (see Box 2007). In particular, it sought to shift the locus of public administration away from efficiency and toward social equity (see Marini 1971; Frederickson 1971). But it also attacked the notion of a value-free public administration and the diminution of politics to its essence. The NPA challenged the administrative behaviorists in that it sought to move public administration study and theory toward postpositivism, where precise measurement and verifiable observation are illusive. For the new public administrationists, it is simply not possible to divorce people and politics from values, ethics, and morality, and hence it is implausible that public administration can be studied objectively.

Another post Waldo–Simon debate emerged in 1973 with an exchange between Chris Argyris and Simon. It appeared in *Public Administration Review*, and couched the philosophy of science question in the context of humanism, which centers on the complex emotive and psychological attributes of humans.[15] Argyris and other humanists maintained that the positivist, value-free, and "rational" methods of studying organizational behavior advanced by behaviorists such as Simon failed to capture the intricacies of human conduct (or misconduct, especially irrationality) and, in effect, failed to advance administrative theory in any significant way. The rational component of human behavior, according to Argyris, was eclipsing its emotional and motivational components. Argyris (1973b, 253) argued:

> Organizational theory in public administration may be undergoing an important transformation. The new critics find much administrative descriptive theory to be nonrelevant to many critical problems of organization. . . . The new stirrings in public administration may be seen as part of a broader intellectual debate that has evolved in the field of organizational behavior. Scholars on both sides of the issue are in agreement that it is important to design organizations that are more effective. One side believes that this can be best accomplished through increasing rationality and descriptive research; the other on increasing humane dimensions and therefore normative research.

Simon (1973b) countered with his philosophy on the nature of evidence, especially the importance of scientific empirical evidence, laced with reason and facts, as compared with "normative activity" and anecdotal evidence for the advancement of organizational theory. He stated: "My mind boggles at how I might reach common ground with Argyris on the nature of evidence. He reacts to empirical data describing a decision process with: 'I found another scenario more plausible.' To which I can only answer with the punchline of an ancient joke: 'Vas you dere Charlie (or Chris)?' . . .

The point simply is that when particular data conflict with a priori feelings of plausibility, the latter must yield" (Simon 1973a, 484).[16] The metaphysical tug of war between Simon and Argyris resulted in the same stalemate, hooded by complementary entrenched positions, as that produced by Simon and Waldo.

IS PUBLIC ADMINISTRATION A SCIENCE?

The debates between Waldo and Simon and between Simon and Argyris over the fact/value dichotomy intersect with the question of whether public administration is an art or science. Lurking behind both debates, we have seen, is the question of the appropriate epistemic traditions for the field (see Riccucci 2006). This issue has both a practical and scholarly component, raising these questions:

1. Is public administration as practiced primarily an art, requiring intuition and experience, or can it can be based on scientifically derived knowledge?
2. Does the search for public administration theory require artful insight, or can it be made wholly scientific?

The debate over the first question begets another question: Are administrators "born" or can they be "made," that is, trained? The development of educational programs for public service in the first half of the twentieth century proceeded from the belief that a body of knowledge could be derived that, when taught to novices, could help them become better executives (see, e.g., Mosher 1975). Yet a contrary belief maintains that innate or "inborn" talents predispose certain persons to become leaders or exemplary managers, meaning that they are "natural-born leaders."

As Simon and others maintained, the futile struggle that characterized the early study of public administration demonstrated that governmental management could not be reduced to easily derived and trainable principles that described "one best way." The practice of public administration continues to require the art-like qualities associated with wisdom and experience. But the practice of public administration also requires scientific training insofar as persons need technical preparation to become public administrators. Few people argue that untrained public servants would on the whole perform as well as people trained in administrative skills. Indeed, the very existence of the master of public administration degree (MPA) represents a scientific and analytic endeavor (never, of course, sans politics). As Leonard White (1929, 1955) tells us, a society that becomes complex and mutable must continually rely on the technical and scientific training of government administrators. The common conception treats the practice of public administration as both art and science.

The second question asks whether public administration, in the scholarly search for theory or understanding, is an art or a science. Due to the inevitable presence of human beings, public administration can never be reduced to certainties such as those found in the natural or physical sciences (e.g., chemistry, astronomy, and physics). Instead, as most would agree, public administration is a branch of the social sciences (see, e.g., Box 1992).

Beyond this simple taxonomy, the resolution of the art/science issue in the study of public administration intersects the perdurable debate over philosophies of science. From ontological and epistemological standpoints, one might approach the question as it is depicted in figure 1.1. Where exactly does public administration fit into this disciplinary framework? Here one can find three identifiable camps. The first group claims that public administration theory can and must be scientific; the second group asserts that it has been, historically, an art and, hence, is value laden; and the third group sees elements of both art/values and science/facts.

The first camp, comprising early behaviorists and more lately people applying economic theories to the analysis of public policies, advocated a logical positivist approach. According to this group, there is no room for the metaphysical speculation, reason, or innate ideas that early rationalists allowed. Rather, the creation of administrative theory must be deductive and based on value-free, rationally derived, testable hypotheses. The goal of knowledge, they insist, is simply to describe the phenomena experienced. Empirically based, quantitative research is the only way, the "one best way," to seek and discover truth and reality. For some in this camp, quantitative data and research method drive ideas, concepts, and theory, rather than vice versa.

The second camp views the study of public administration as an art. For the members of this group, metaphysical concerns have a prominent place in administrative research and theory building. They leave room for reasoning, dialectic, and induction, and research that can be descriptive— even empirically so—prescriptive, and normative. The chief source of knowledge, they argue, is reason. As noted above, the new public administration, reacting in the late 1960s against the behavioral movement in public administration, is representative of this coterie (see Marini 1971).

Figure 1.1 A Disciplinary Continuum: From Science to Art

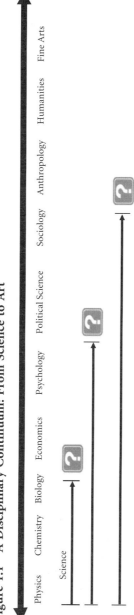

Source: Adapted from Dempster 1998.

The third group in public administration sees the field as both art and science (see, e.g., Raadschelders 1999). Given the variegated and applied nature of the field, they maintain, public administrative research should be pluralistic (e.g., see Ventriss 1989). In their view, room exists not only for logical positivism and metaphysical speculation but also for realism, relativism, rationalism, postmodernism, and even reductionism[17] (see Fernández-Armesto 1997; Kitcher 2001). For this camp, there is no one best way to do research, and given the lack of a unified theory, public administration should not strive for an "appropriate" methodology. As Frederickson has suggested, the field can greatly benefit from "a rapprochement between the . . . administrative sciences and the humanities." He goes on to say: "The analytical tools of social sciences help us *know* how organizations operate and how public managers function. But to know public organizations and their management is not to understand them. Understanding requires perspective, experience, judgment, and the capacity to imagine. These qualities have less to do with analytical skills and more to do with philosophy, language, art, and reason" (Frederickson 2000, 51–52). For this group, a diversity of methods is the key to the acquisition of knowledge, perspective, and truth (see, e.g., Raadschelders 2005; Stivers 2000; White and Adams 1994a, 1994b; Adams 1992).

CONCLUSION

The Waldo–Simon debates were instrumental at the time in the development of public administrative theory. They led to further questions about whether public administration did or did not have a paradigmatic base, which is the subject of chapter 2. These dialectical exchanges helped to significantly push the field further in its evolution as one of scientific inquiry. Interestingly enough, however, the same old exchanges perdure today. A series of commentaries appearing in such journals as *Administration and Society*, *Public Administration Review*, and *Administration Theory and Praxis* have been inflammatory, sometimes offensive, and, perhaps due to a smidgen of obstinate hubris, intellectually futile.[18] They are counterproductive, they add little to what Waldo and Simon set forth in the 1950s, and thus they have contributed only marginally to the evolution of knowledge and theory in the field.

Indeed, the dogmatic persistence of particular research traditions has been detrimental to theory building in public administration. Bozeman (2007, 1–2) addresses this issue in the context of public interest theory:

"The reasons for a decline in public interest argument and theorizing are many and varied. Social and academic fashion seems to have played a role. The development of quantitative social sciences and its inexhaustible demand for empirical evidence lessened our patience for topics that seem to hold little possibility of precise answers. The harshest critics of public interest theory rail loudest about its ambiguities and a seeming inability to determine when and if public interest theory has progressed."

These contemporary debates on the supremacy of one research tradition over another have resulted in a metaphysical dyspepsia, and ultimately a Balkanization of knowledge. They will not be regurgitated here. My goal is to emulsify the various epistemic traditions and quite simply help us turn the page.

NOTES

1. It should be noted at the outset that this book accepts as fact the existence of public administration as a field or discipline. This issue had been subjected to heated debates over the course of public administration's history; see, e.g., Waldo 1980. The two terms, field and discipline, will be used interchangeably hereafter.

2. See Raadschelders (1999) for a review of the identity crisis of public administration in Europe.

3. The lack of a coherent, core theory relates to the question of public administration's paradigmatic basis, which is addressed in chapter 2.

4. Some argue that qualitative research (e.g., cross-case comparisons) is mainly for theory building and quantitative research (e.g., multiple regression analysis) is for theory testing. This distinction is not made in this book, which holds that qualitative and quantitative research can both build and test theory. See Kenworthy 2008; and the discussion in chapter 4, esp. n. 3.

5. As Stillman (1999) points out, the self-conscious study of public administration occurred much earlier in other countries such as France.

6. See White 1929; Willoughby 1927; Fayol 1916, 1917, 1937.

7. It also articulated the importance of decision making as a sine qua non of public administration in practice.

8. It should be noted, however, that in his later teachings around artificial intelligence, Simon suggested that it might be possible to find rational decision makers. He is considered to be one of the cofounders of the field of artificial intelligence, whereby computers and computer programs can be relied on to perform functions normally associated with human intelligence. But artificial intelligence goes further to suggest that the computer programs can perform with greater intelligence than human action, particularly around reasoning and optimization. See Simon 1995; Simon and Kadane 1975.

9. Logical empiricism is sometimes used synonymously with logical positivism. This approach is not adopted here. For a discussion, see Hardcastle 2005.

10. Waldo also advanced a democratic theory of public administration in his book *The Administrative State*, which was based on his dissertation at Yale University. And Waldo, like Simon, also challenged various aspects of classical public administration theory such as POSDCORB (planning, organizing, staffing, directing, coordinating, reporting, and budgeting), advanced by Luther Gulick (1937) in "Notes on the Theory of Organization," as universal functions of all administrators.

11. It should be noted that Waldo (1965, 11) treats "pragmatism" as empiricism, or as he later refers to it, a "garden variety" of positivism.

12. Waldo (1984, 171) went on to say that "it is submitted that the established techniques of science are inapplicable to thinking and valuing human beings." However, when he revisited these arguments in 1965, he stated that this was a "half-truth," confessing that "it is simply not the way I would now put and argue my opinions" (Waldo 1965, 13).

13. Peter Drucker's (1952) participation and commentary in the initial debate was eclipsed by the acrimony between Waldo and Simon. Drucker's commentary does not engage the issue of science, but rather addressed the concept of democracy from an industrial or large organization perspective.

14. For a review of the various issues, see Harmon 1989.

15. See Argyris 1973a, 1973b; Simon 1973a, 1973b.

16. In the 1930s, a radio program featured an actor, Jack Pearl, portraying the part of "Baron Munchausen." During the program, someone would question his outlandish stories, at which point he would ask in jest: "Vas you dere, Charlie?"

17. These concepts will be elaborated upon in chapter 4.

18. See, e.g., Luton 2007a; Lynn, Heinrich, and Hill 2008; Spicer 2007. Some of these commentaries appear in books, e.g., Lynn 1996. But see Raadschelders 2005, who admirably calls for an acceptance of methodological pluralism; also see White and Adams 1994a, 1994b.

Searching for a Paradigm

PUBLIC ADMINISTRATION AS A POSTNORMAL SCIENCE

A **related question** as to whether public administration is based on fact, value, or characterized by art or science is, Does public administration have a paradigm? Public administrationists have similarly grappled with this issue, at least since Thomas Kuhn's (1962) classic *The Structure of Scientific Revolutions*. The term "paradigm" had heretofore largely been used in certain forms of linguistics. For example, it was applied to the various patterns one learned to sort or conjugate verbs. Thus in the Italian language, a paradigm for the (irregular) verb "to be" or "essere" is

Io sono	(I am)
tu sei	(you are)
lei/lui è	(she/he is)
noi siamo	(we are)
voi siete	(you are, plural)
loro sono	(they are)

Beginning in the 1960s the term "paradigm" was used in science in the very broad or universal sense to refer to a theoretical framework. The 1975 Nobel laureate in medicine, David Baltimore, cited the work of two colleagues that "really established a new paradigm for our understanding of the causation of cancer" (*American Heritage Guide* 2005, 341). But it was Thomas Kuhn who in 1962 created a stir about the existence of paradigms in scientific communities, seeking to provide a more particularized conceptualization of the term. Because public administration had been seen by many as a community of "science," à la Herbert Simon and other behaviorists, the question of public administration's paradigmatic basis was launched.

This chapter begins with a cursory review of Kuhn's *The Structure of Scientific Revolutions*. It then follows with a discussion of the various commentaries by public administrationists on the existence of a paradigm, or the lack thereof. Because Kuhn conceptualized paradigms in the context of the hard or physical sciences, other accounts of the inability of public administration to achieve paradigmatic status are presented, including the applied nature of the field. The chapter examines the question of whether public administration can ever be studied as a normal science—for example, in the Kuhnian context—or if it is better classified as a postnormal science.

KUHN, PARADIGMS, AND NORMAL SCIENCE

When Thomas Kuhn was a graduate student studying physics at Harvard University, he began to probe the history of science as he was teaching an undergraduate course. In his studies, he stumbled upon the conundrum of the marked disparities between Aristotelian and Newtonian physics. Why, he wondered, were the two models, both based in the natural science of physics, at complete odds with one another? He concluded that Newtonian physics could not have emerged in any conceivable way from Aristotelian physics—so there must have been a revolution in thinking (Crotty 1998, 34).

This experience led to the primary thesis of Kuhn's book: Science progresses through cycles, evolving not gradually and cumulatively toward truth, but through periodic, radical revolutions or paradigm shifts. Although Kuhn used the term "paradigm" in twenty-one distinct senses, a distillation of his usages suggests that a paradigm is the model that governs scientific inquiry in a discipline at any given time.[1] There is a shared commitment to such a paradigm among the members of the scientific community, which is bound to its discipline by mutual beliefs concerning theoretical constructs, epistemology, and methodologies. Thus, according to Kuhn, a paradigm is essential to scientific inquiry and progress.

During a period of "normal science" scholars or scientists engage in the routine task of "puzzle solving" or scientific inquiry; they are governed by their existing paradigm. A scientific revolution occurs when scientists encounter anomalies that cannot be explained by the universally accepted paradigm that has heretofore guided their scientific inquiries. There is a "recognition that nature has somehow violated the paradigm-induced expectations that govern normal science" (Kuhn 1996, 52–53). The period of normal science is replaced by a scientific revolution, thus producing a shift in the commitment to shared assumptions—that is, to the paradigm itself.

For Kuhn a mature science develops through successive transitions from one paradigm to another through this process of revolutions. Once a revolution has occurred and the paradigm has shifted, the field is once again returned to the period or cycle of normal science until another anomaly and then revolution occur.

Kuhn offers several examples of this process, including that of scientific revolutions in physics. He explains that the early science of physics was governed by various theories or laws advanced by Aristotle in the fourth century BC. Aristotle's theory of gravity, for example, held that all bodies move toward their natural place, either the Earth or the heavens. So any object thrown into the air would always return to the ground. This was the governing paradigm during the period of normal science. A scientific revolution occurred when Newton advanced his universal law of gravity, which provided a mathematical formula for gravitational force; it established that the force that causes an apple to fall back to the Earth is the same as that which keeps planets in their orbits. According to Aristotelian thought, the planets were believed to remain in their orbits as a result of divine intervention. Thus a new paradigmatic basis for gravitational force replaced the paradigm under which Aristotelian scientific inquiry was conducted. Another scientific revolution occurred with Einstein's theory of general relativity, which superseded Newtonian law.[2]

Kuhn concludes that scientific communities are often reluctant and resistant to change, where the old ways of "doing" are replaced with new ways. However, as he argues, change is necessary in that it represents scientific progress in any given field or discipline. For a scientific community to embrace change, Kuhn (1996, 169) argues that two conditions must be met: "First, the new candidate [for paradigm] must seem to resolve some outstanding and generally recognized problem that can be met in no other way. Second, the new paradigm must promise to preserve a relatively large part of the concrete problem-solving ability that has accrued to science through its predecessors."

DOES PUBLIC ADMINISTRATION HAVE A PARADIGM?

If we think of paradigms in a broad sense—as models, worldviews, bodies of thought, or even, as Kuhn (1996, 10) propounded, as that which "attract(s) an enduring group of adherents"—then a paradigmatic base guides public administration. Moreover, most would agree that other attributes of a paradigm, from a Kuhnian perspective, apply to public administration. For example, public administration has specialized journals, professional societies or specialized groups, discussion groups and listservs, and its own place in the academy.[3]

Lan and Anders (2000, 162) make the case that public administration does have a paradigm, because there is "a set of tacitly agreed-upon paradigms that guide public administration research. The foremost governing paradigm is publicness," a dimension or quality developed by Bozeman (1987), which is aimed at determining the degree to which "public authority" affects or influences organizations; the concept is intended to help distinguish public from private organizations. Lan and Anders (2000, 155, 162) argue that this paradigm "asserts that public administration differs from other types of management, private management in particular, in meaningful ways. . . . Under this umbrella, a set of subparadigms (approaches) are competing with one another in guiding the inquiries of researchers. Insofar as paradigms have profound conditioning influences on what scholars think, an important step in advancing the conduct of inquiry in public administration is to become conscious of these underlying paradigms that govern knowledge development and research in the field."

Others have tacitly accepted this casual definition of paradigm without questioning its relevancy from a research or "scientific" perspective. For example, in a leading public administration textbook, *Public Administration and Public Affairs*, Nicholas Henry (2006) refers to "paradigms" of public administration as the various intellectual periods defining the field's development. For example, the "orthodox" paradigm refers to the dominance of scientific management and the discipline's preoccupation with discovering principles of administration that would ensure efficiency, effectiveness, and economy in government operations.

Most recently Lynn (2001) and a number of others have also relied on the term "paradigm" more casually to question whether a paradigmatic shift from the traditional or "Weberian" bureaucracy to "new public management" has occurred.[4] Some use the term "paradigm" to represent theoretical lenses that share various approaches to inquiry (Yang, Zhang, and Holzer 2008).

However, Rommel and Christiaens (2006, 610) go so far as to say that public administrationists have complacently bandied the term "paradigm" about in a reckless, illogical manner. They maintain that "traditional scholars . . . use the paradigm concept too loosely, thereby only leading to heated scholarly discussions and 'paradigm wars' but not resulting in practical or useful answers." They essentially argue: How can there be a paradigmatic shift, when no paradigm existed in the first place?

In a very strict sense, especially Kuhnian, most would concur that public administration lacks a governing paradigmatic base. Rainey (1994, 41, 48), for example, argues that "we have no paradigm," but he goes on to say that "there is a degree of consensus . . . on the validity and value of a focus on the public sector as a domain of inquiry." From a pure science perspective, we do not and cannot have a paradigmatic base, as Rainey aptly points out.

Other factors also help explain why public administration lacks a paradigm. For example, public administration is an applied field. Public administration is concerned with applying scientific knowledge to solve practical problems in highly politicized environments. The real world of government and nonprofits is our laboratory; we do not bring subjects or specimens into a lab as the physical sciences do. Most of our research is conducted in the "field," and it is aimed at improving government or, more specifically, arriving at a better understanding of it so we can seek to improve governing operations in this country and beyond. But because politics drives performance in public agencies, our understanding of government and how it operates in practice are in a constant state of flux.

Moreover, public-sector environments are driven by multiple, politically driven norms. For example, governments must work to manage the public's tax dollars in an efficient and economical manner. However, they are regulated by legal mandates that invariably affect their behaviors and actions, which may ultimately lead to inefficient outcomes (see Rosenbloom 1983a, 1983b). Which values are or should be dominant? Managerial or legal? Efficiency or the legal and constitutional rights of the bureaucracy's workers or clients? As Moynihan (2009, 820) points out: "The juggling of multiple values makes the lives of both administrative practitioners and scholars more complex. It may have limited the capacity of scholarship to define and build on core doctrinal beliefs in the way that economics has. But all social science disciplines, including economics, have become more fragmented over time. The reactive nature of public administration also creates a danger of ceaseless pursuit of the latest fashions. . . . But strip away the faddish language of many reforms, and we see a remarkable continuity in terms of their underlying values."

In practice, then, there cannot be a single, dominant value or norm. In effect, the task of public administration will always revolve around practical applications of solving problems in the real world, which is highly political, fragmented, and transitory.

Another reason why public administration is not able to achieve paradigmatic status is related to its multidisciplinary nature. It draws from a host of fields or disciplines, such as political science, law, business, sociology, and economics. Although public administration is inexorably integrated by these recognizable parts, its multidisciplinary nature, as Waldo (1980, 61) maintains, prevents it from developing an "indisputable paradigm and an agreed methodology."

Notwithstanding, as a community of scholars, we do not like to admit that the field is not capable of achieving a paradigm, because that admission might serve to marginalize or lessen public administration as a discipline or scholarly endeavor. Indeed, as Kuhn makes clear in one of his many usages of the construct, paradigms help scientific communities to bind their discipline; pre-paradigmatic disciplines, he purports, are "immature sciences." Thus public administration has sought to identify or formulate—albeit futilely—a governing paradigmatic base.

Kuhn (1996, 161, emphasis added) also argued that questions about whether a field or discipline is a paradigm-driven science "will cease to be a source of concern *not* when a definition is found, but when the groups that now doubt their own status achieve consensus about their past and present accomplishments." There may be consensus on a number of issues, including public administration's past and present achievements, and that it is punctuated by various intellectual developments or movements.

However, dissension arises with respect to the importance or *significance* of those contributions, developments, and movements, particularly when evaluated from the standpoint of methodology. Dissonance has been seen most vividly over the Waldo–Simon debates, and who prevailed. Bertelli and Lynn (2006, 46, 48, 179n.13), for example, take quite a few digs at Waldo's accomplishment, particularly in comparison with Simon's. They suggest that unlike Simon, Waldo was a one-trick pony, unable to move on to new intellectual ground after *The Administrative State*. Also, again evaluating Simon against Waldo, they point out that Simon as well as Robert Dahl "went on to establish themselves as among the finest social scientist of their generation" (Bertelli and Lynn 2006, 48). They go on to say that "it is Simon who was awarded the American Society for Public Administration's Dwight Waldo Award, not vice versa" (Bertelli and Lynn (2006, 48).

Bertelli and Lynn (2006, 48) classify Waldo as a postmodernist and antipositivist. Referencing the works of others, they see him as "a practitioner of hermeneutics," with a "humanistic-literary bias" and "intimations of Derrida and deconstructionism." Citing Taylor's (2004) op-ed commentary in the *New York Times*, they argue that "'the guiding insight of deconstruction . . . is that every structure—be it literary, psychological, social, economic, political or religious—that organizes our experiences is constituted and maintained through acts of exclusion. In the process of creating something, [something] else inevitably gets left out. These exclusive structures can become repressive—and that repression comes with consequences. . . . What is repressed does not disappear but always returns to unsettle every construction, no matter how secure it seems.' While Waldo never puts the matter so clearly, this formulation may well sum up his worldview."

Conversely, many scholars have acknowledged Waldo's salient contributions to the field. For example, Rosenbloom and McCurdy (2006, ix, 1, 4) state that Waldo's *The Administrative State* "fundamentally changed the study of public administration, presumably forever" and that it has achieved "iconic status." They praise Waldo as one of the leading figures in public administration.[5] They go on to say that "the rich literature on the relationship of bureaucracy to democracy, representative bureaucracy, participatory bureaucracy, grassroots administration and related topics that developed after 1948 owes much of its intellectual origins to Waldo's work. . . . By the 1950s, Waldo was widely recognized as a major public administration thinker. From the late 1950s, if not earlier, through the 1970s, he was generally considered the leading academic in the field."

Some have even dedicated their books to him. Rosenbloom (1988a) did so with the first edition of his public administration text, *Public Administration: Understanding Management, Politics and Law in the Public Sector*. So, too, did Stillman (1991), in *Preface to Public Administration: A Search for Themes and Directions*.

As alluded to in chapter 1, the battle lines among contemporary scholars about the field's scientificity and whose contributions are more estimable, Waldo's or Simon's, are drawn in stone. Thus there is no consensus in the field on a particular school of thought or methodology.

Another critical point, as mentioned above, is that Kuhn's contextual framework, as well as all the examples he raises in his book, are grounded in the natural or physical sciences. He repeatedly points to Newtonian mechanics, Einsteinian dynamics, and Copernican cosmology to support his premise that paradigmatic disciplines are mature sciences. He also stated that without a commitment to a paradigm, there could be no normal science. Perhaps his hidden subtext was that only the natural sciences are or can be paradigmatic and, hence, characterized as normal sciences.

Public administration, then, as with any of the other branches of the social sciences, can only be preparadigmatic or nonparadigmatic because no single paradigm exists or has emerged during the stages of scientific inquiry. Moreover, according to Kuhn, only paradigmatic disciplines can be classified as "mature," normal sciences. If we accept these premises, then a preparadigmatic or nonparadigmatic discipline such as public administration cannot be a normal, paradigm-governed science, but may be better taxonomized as a "postnormal science."

PUBLIC ADMINISTRATION AS A POSTNORMAL SCIENCE

"Postnormal science" is a concept conceived and articulated by Funtowicz and Ravetz (1992, 1993, 1994) to address the existence of societal and ethical complexities in the environments we study. A postnormal science is a process of inquiry for which objectivity is not always achievable. Environmental factors, particularly politics, interfere with the quest for objectivity, and, consequently, prediction and control are limited. A postnormal science, according to Funtowicz and Ravetz, is one that is relevant when high risks, uncertainty, and divergent values prevail. It urges new methods in the development and application of scientific knowledge, an extended peer community (i.e., one where a dialogue is created among all stakeholders, regardless of their official position or qualifications), and an "extension" of facts (Sardar 2000; Dempster 1998). Funtowicz and Ravetz (1992, 254), in effect, have called for a broader conception of science, or "the democratization of science."

Of particular importance, the postnormal sciences operate with a different level of assumptions as compared with the normal sciences. For instance, unlike the normal sciences, which are assumed to be both certain and value free, postnormal science, as Ravetz (1999, 647) points out, "makes 'systems uncertainties' and 'decision stakes' the essential elements of its analysis." He goes on to say that the

> insight leading to Post-Normal Science is that in the sorts of issue-driven science relating to environmental debates, typically facts are uncertain, values in dispute, stakes high, and decisions urgent. Some might say that such problems should not be called 'science'; but the answer could be that such problems are everywhere, and when science is (as it must be) applied to them, the conditions are anything but "normal." For the previous distinction between "hard," objective scientific facts and "soft," subjective value judgments is now inverted. All too often, we must make hard policy decisions where our only scientific inputs are irremediably soft. In such contexts of

policy making, there is a new role for natural science. The facts that are taught from textbooks in institutions are still necessary, but are no longer sufficient. For these relate to a standardised version of the natural world, frequently to the artificially pure and stable conditions of a laboratory experiment. The world is quite different when we interact with it, either destructively or constructively. . . . Contrary to the impression conveyed by textbooks, most problems in practice have more than one plausible answer, and many have no answer at all. (Ravetz 1999, 649)

Funtowicz and Ravetz (2008) characterize environmental policy as a postnormal science. They acknowledge that the environment is in the domain of "science," given its immersion in the world of nature. But they go on to say that we have never been nor ever will be the "masters and possessors of Nature." The uncertainty and complexity of the environment warrant the use of new intellectual tools to study the structure and properties of the phenomena underlying environmental problems. They argue for linking epistemological stances with suitable methods but, most important, they call for pluralist representations of knowledge. They reject the narrow conception of positivism as the one best way and instead call for approaches that are broader and more inclusive of different epistemic traditions and methodologies.

Postnormal science has been applied to a number of different fields, including ecological economics (Swedeen 2006; Muller 2003), food safety (Ravetz 2002), medicine (Sweeney and Kernick 2002; Laugharne and Laugharne 2002), and climate science (Bray and von Storch 1999; Saloranta 2001). In all these fields, research and action depend upon value-laden decisions that are inescapably made in the face of uncertainty. Postnormal science moves beyond traditional research, where certainties prevail, to a method where the quality of the research process is primary (see Turnpenny 2003).

If public administration cannot be characterized as normal science, perhaps postnormal science is a more fitting classification. If this is the case, what should its approach to research be? How should scientific inquiry be carried out? How do the various approaches to research postulate reality and truth, and by what means do we arrive at the truth in public administration—or, more broadly, the social sciences? Is it "scientific" methods that lead us to the truth? And what exactly constitute methods grounded in "science?" How will we know if or when we have arrived at the truth?

Before turning to these questions in chapter 4, the next chapter examines the issues of identity crises and paradigmatic bases in the other social sciences, illustrating that public administration is not unique in its constant quest for an "identity."

NOTES

1. See Rainey 1994; Lakatos and Musgrave 1970.

2. It should be noted, however, that given the circumscribed conditions for which relativity is applicable or suitable, (e.g., when extreme accuracy is a prerequisite or when dealing with gravitation for very massive objects), Newton's Law continues to be used as an excellent approximation of the effects of gravity.

3. Of course, public administration can "belong" to departments, programs, or schools of public administration, public affairs, public policy, political science, business administration, etc. This exacerbates the "identity" conundrum in the field.

4. See Kuhlmann, Bogumil, and Grohs 2008; Page 2005; Cheung 2005; Gow and Dufour 2000; Borins 1999; Mathiasen 1999; Aucoin 1995.

5. Rosenbloom and McCurdy's (2006) edited book emanated from a symposium they organized at American University to commemorate Waldo's *The Administrative State*.

Identity Crises in the Social Sciences

Public administration is not the only social science that has grappled with questions of identity and the significance of paradigms (see, e.g., Dubnick 1999). Other social sciences have also subjected their research traditions to epistemological and ontological gauntlets in search of a paradigmatic base or precise identity through which to promote scientific rigor or "science" in their respective fields or disciplines. These debates have predominantly revolved around epistemic traditions and research methodology, and not surprisingly have pitted positivism against postpositivism—which acknowledges the value of qualitative methodologies—or other philosophies of science. As Rosenberg (2008, 1) points out, "There is no perfect agreement among economists, anthropologists, sociologists, or psychologists on what the distinctive and central problems and methods of their respective disciplines are."

To avoid tedium and repetition, given the epistemological debates in public administration presented earlier in this volume, this chapter provides only a brief overview of the discourse in other social sciences concerned with identity and paradigms. But an important point to be made is that even those branches of the social sciences (e.g., political science and sociology) that are not applied or as closely identified with practice as public administration struggle with questions of identity, paradigmatic base, and appropriate research methodology.

POLITICAL SCIENCE

In political science, intellectual squabbles over aims and research methods have long peppered the discourse (e.g., Brady and Collier 2004; deLeon 1998; Ellwood 1996; King, Keohane, and Verba 1994; Weimer 1992; Gunnell 1991; Ricci 1984). Many have argued that political science is more a behavioral science (i.e., a quantitatively empirical undertaking), whereas others have maintained that it is systematic thought about politics (i.e., ethics, morality, and values). Perhaps deLeon (1998, 150) succinctly captured the factiousness as follows: "Political scientists as a discipline have spent (almost literally) countless articles and books proposing something resembling 'laws' or theories that, taken collectively or individually, have produced infinitely more confusion than clarity." To bolster his case, deLeon juxtaposes the works of a number of eminent political science philosophers, such as James Rosenau and Charles Lindblom. As deLeon (1998, 150) points out, Rosenau saw the primary purpose of political science as moving "up the ladder of generalization and construct[ing] theories that encompass and explain more and more of the phenomena that make up the universe of politics." Lindblom (1990), conversely, questioned the utility of *any* social science findings for social tasks or efforts.

As with public administration, political scientists line both sides of the gauntlet, arguing that political behavior is best understood through explanatory techniques (the positivists) or through reason, description, or prescription. Torgerson (1986, 34), for example, argues that positivism "would rigorously distance itself from the speculations of theology and metaphysics, confronting the world objectively in order to observe the facts and determine the lawful order of nature and society. The domain of mystery and ambiguity would be abandoned in order to know what could be known clearly and certainly. . . . Knowledge would replace politics." Others, such as deLeon (1998, 151), counter that "positivism is fundamentally antithetical to democratic principles and processes. Another claim is that, in its search for objectivity, it conveniently overlooks the pivotal hurly-burly of political life, and especially the contending value structures."[1]

Some political scientists have argued that qualitative research encompasses positivism. Lin (1998, 162), for example, takes this position, arguing that "positivist work seeks to identify qualitative data with propositions that can then be tested or identified in other cases. . . . Qualitative work can be positivist: It can attempt to document practices that lead consistently to one set of outcomes rather than another, to identify characteristics that commonly are related to some policy problem, or to find strategic patterns that hold across different venues and with different actors."[2]

As with public administration, myriad treatises can be offered to illustrate the dialectical exchanges over scope and methods of political science (e.g., compare King, Keohane, and Verba 1994 with Brady and Collier 2004).[3] Moreover, similar to public administration, some, like Elman (2008, 272) argue that political science has "outgrown a one-size-fits-all approach and can be seen to encompass a rich diversity" of approaches, especially mixed methods. Elman goes on to say that political science should not "follow a single-logic-of-inference model" based in positivism. Similarly, Brady and Collier (2004, xvii) also argue for diversity in research approaches: "Crafting good social science research requires diverse methodological tools. Such tools include a variety of qualitative and quantitative approaches: small-N and large-N analyses, case studies and structural equation modeling, ethnographic field research and quantitative natural experiments, close analysis of meaning and large-scare surveys." In the end, as deLeon (1998, 150) offers, it comes down to this: "Even within the political science community, there is genuine question as to whether many of its theories are universally (or even widely) accepted, which casts some question as to its ascription of 'science.'"

THE POLICY SCIENCES

There is a persistent debate over the identity of the policy sciences, a movement or field that does not seem to have any precise definition. The term "policy sciences" was coined by the U.S. political scientist Harold Lasswell, who was seeking a better way to address policy problems within a democratic framework.[4] To Lasswell, any discipline or profession with relevance to government could be described as a policy science (deLeon 1997; Lasswell 1951). deLeon (1988, 7) refers to "policy sciences" as "an umbrella term describing a broad-gauge intellectual approach applied to the examination of societally critical problems. . . . The policy sciences, as we shall see, are problem-oriented and contextual in nature, multidisciplinary in approach, and explicitly normative in perspective. They represent a variety of approaches to understanding and resolving issues of great public importance."

Parenthetically, as deLeon (1988, 8) maintains, policy analysis "is the most noted derivative and application of the tools and methodologies of the policy sciences' approach. . . . Policy analysis is generally considered a more discrete genus under the broader umbrella of the policy sciences phylum. Quite often and unfortunately, they are used interchangeably."

Pielke (2004, 215) explicitly argues that the "policy sciences lack a distinctive identity within the policy movement, in spite of a journal, a professional society and a website (www.policysciences.org)." Moreover, his Internet search, conducted in 2004, could not identify a single graduate program called "policy sciences." Instead, he found such programs as policy studies, policy analysis, and public affairs.

Not only the scope but also the methods of policy sciences have undergone rigorous critiques. In an incisive essay examining policy sciences' neopositivist (or logical positivist) approach, Fischer (1998, 129–30) states: "Not only is neopositivist policy science seen to have failed in its effort to develop a usable body of predictive generalizations, it has been unable to supply effective solutions to social problems. An important part of this failure is traced to outmoded epistemological assumptions. . . . In the policy sciences the attempt to separate facts and values has facilitated a technocratic form of policy analysis that emphasizes the efficiency and effectiveness of means to achieve politically established goals." In short the same debates in public administration about identity, facts, values, and methodology permeate other fields such as the policy sciences and the closely related field of policy analysis.

POLICY ANALYSIS

Policy analysis evolved from such areas or fields as administrative science, management science, systems engineering, and operations research. It has assumed a host of different meanings, especially in the context of public administration (see, e.g., Denhardt 2004). And as with public administration, theory and practice have become so inextricably linked that it is virtually impossible to separate the identity of policy analysis as a profession from its academic underpinnings. It burst on the scene of public administration in about the 1960s as an action-oriented discipline designed to promote greater responsiveness to social needs through public policies (see, e.g., Henry 2006; Stillman 1991; Frederickson and Smith 2003).[5]

Policy analysis, too, suffers from a personality disorder. Some equate it with policy studies, policy evaluation, policy planning, program evaluation, or even public affairs (e.g., Pielke 2004). deLeon, as noted above, sees policy analysis as a methodological derivative of the policy sciences. He has also argued that "systems analysis" is often confused with policy analysis because of its reliance on quantitative tools and applications to address policy problems (deLeon 1988). The political scientist Thomas Dye (1976) also viewed policy analysis as empirically based methods, as opposed to normative ones, for the accumulation of knowledge about political processes.

IDENTITY CRISES IN THE SOCIAL SCIENCES

In *Beyond Machiavelli: Policy Analysis Comes of Age*, Beryl Radin (2000, 5–6) presents a host of different definitions of policy analysis, including these:

♦ Policy analysis is a multi-element process of assessing and analyzing the components that make up the stated "policy," or plan of action.

♦ Policy analysis is not an exact science but rather an art. There are numerous approaches one can take within policy analysis. One is to establish an agenda, then formulate the issues, address alternatives, set the adoption and implementation plans, and then establish a feedback vehicle.

♦ Policy analysis is the utilization of applied techniques, formal and informal, to arrive at one recommendation for the benefit of a client based on a prescribed policy.

It appears that one's orientation toward policy analysis varies from a disciplinary standpoint; indeed, policy analysis programs are housed in a number of different departments or schools: public administration, political science, economics, sociology, organization studies, and even business administration. This further contributes to the identity quandary.

In common parlance policy analysis as an academic endeavor tends to be equated with economic analysis and research methods. A number of scholars and researchers, including deLeon and Dye, interpret policy analysis as a discipline that is dominated by the perspective of positivist social science. Torgerson (1986, 35) argues that "policy analysis today bears the unmistakable imprint of the positivist heritage. . . . In the case of policy analysis, the influence of positivism has been pervasive not only in letter, but also in spirit."

Others, however, resist and eschew the pull of policy analysis toward quantitative empiricism and positivism. Indeed a number of eminent scholars of policy analysis—such as Beryl Radin, Aaron Wildavsky, Peter deLeon, Dvora Yanow, Eugene Bardach, Yehezkel Dror, and Thomas Kaplan, to name a few—continue an epistemic tradition grounded in qualitative empiricism.[6] And, as Durning (1999, 393) argued, "It is a mistake to portray the founders of [policy analysis] or the present leaders of the intellectual infrastructure of the discipline, as methodological zealots who have ignored other aspects of policy analysis." Quoting Quade (1975), Durning states: "'No public policy question can be answered by analysis alone, divorced from political considerations; judgment and intuition play a large role.'"

In short, as with public administration, no paradigm or single perspective governs policy analysis.

PUBLIC MANAGEMENT AND THE NEW PUBLIC MANAGEMENT

Public management and the new public management have not generally been viewed as separate disciplinary fields of the social sciences. However, they are addressed here precisely because of the identity quagmire that engulfs these areas of study and practice.[7] In fact some do not make distinctions between public management and public administration (e.g., Pollitt and Bouckaert 2000; Evans and Wamsley 1999), viewing management and administration as tantamount. Others see public management as a subset of public administration (e.g., Kettl and Milward 1996; Ott, Hyde, and Shafritz 1991).

Public management has taken on a variety of meanings especially in terms of practice (see, e.g., Hood 2007; Brudney, O'Toole, and Rainey 2000; Frederickson 1999; Fountain 1994; Bozeman 1993). For example, Allison (1979, 38) refers to public management as the direction and organization of such resources as personnel and financial in government to achieve desired ends. He also argued that "public management as a field of knowledge should start from problems faced by practicing public managers." Other eminent scholars of public management—including Cam Stivers, Hal Rainey, Beryl Radin, Bob Behn, Pat Ingraham, Don Kettl, and Christopher Hood, to name a few—have added their own mark to the field's theoretical core.[8] From the standpoint of practice, they have asked, for example, "What do public managers do?" or "How can public management be effectively practiced?" Public managers have been classified as policymakers, program developers, performance auditors, public executives, political strategists, and directors of budgets and human resources management. Their purpose is to improve the operation of government from the standpoint of efficiency, accountability, responsiveness, democratic organization, and the law (Rosenbloom 1983b, 1988a). There are simply innumerable accounts of what public management is or ought to be, as a profession or academic enterprise.[9]

Kettl and Milward (1996, vii, 5) explicitly state that there is no precise definition of public management: "Public management has long been a field in search of structure. Its scholars and practitioners know what it is not: It is neither traditional public administration nor policy analysis. It borrows heavily from a host of disciplines. . . . It is self-evidently important." They go on to say that as competing academic disciplines have sought to lay claim to it, the "study of public management sometimes can resemble less an accumulation of knowledge and more a family feud."

Brudney, O'Toole, and Rainey (2000, 4) argue that "during the 1980s numerous prominent scholars with a variety of academic orientations began to converge on a new topic called 'public management.'" Distinct groups defined public management differently. For example, some see it as "normative discourse about such matters as administrative responsibility, ethics and social equity." Brudney and his colleagues go on to say that another group linked to business administration approaches public management more generically, viewing it in the context of organizational theory and behavior, human resources management, and strategic management. A third group of scholars, mainly from public policy programs, views it as an executive policymaking and strategic leadership function.[10]

From the standpoint of theory, the question shifts to "How do we study what public managers do?" But like public administration, the more urgent and divisive question is "What is the *best* way to study public management?"[11] The advent of public management resembles the arrival of behaviorism in public administration. In the 1970s and 1980s newly formed schools of public policy at Harvard and Princeton universities, among others, assumed the name public management to promote strategic thinking about, for example, the public policy process. According to this train of thought, public managers ought to behave in a rational, strategic manner.

The movement of public management from a theoretical perspective can partly be viewed as a repudiation of normative techniques in public administration, perhaps in response to the new public administration. As discussed in chapter 1, the new public administration, reacting critically to the forces of behaviorism in public administration, sought to promote a normative public administration (see Frederickson 1996).[12] In a veritable tug of war, those scholars branded as public management specialists, or at least a faction of them, sought to maintain a positivist focus to public administration, as introduced by the behaviorists. If public administration was to be mired in a morass of metaphysics, hermeneutics, and phenomenology, then a coterie of scholars would hang their hats in the emergent field of public management and classify it as a positivist enterprise. This is not to say that the entire field of public management can be portrayed in this fashion. On the contrary, notable scholars—Bob Behn, Pat Ingraham, Beryl Radin, George Frederickson, Barbara Romzek, Geert Bouckaert, and Don Kettl, to name a few—demonstrate analytical rigor in a postpositivist, qualitative tradition.

The new public management (NPM) is another development in public administration or public management, and it, too, lacks a consensus over its boundaries or identity. The term was coined by Christopher Hood (1991), who initially conceived of the NPM as a convergence of management, production engineering, and public choice theory. He stated that the "NPM, like most administrative labels, is a loose term. Its usefulness lies in its convenience as a shorthand name for the set of broadly similar administrative doctrines which dominated the bureaucratic reform agenda in many of the OECD [Organization for Economic Cooperation and Development] group of countries from the late 1970s" (Hood 1991, 3–4). He went on to say that the NPM represented a "marriage of two different streams of ideas. One partner was the 'new institutional economies.' It was built on the now very familiar story of the post–World War II development of public choice, transactions cost theory and principal–agent theory. . . . The other partner in the 'marriage' was the latest of a set of successive waves of business-type 'managerialism' in the public sector, in the tradition of the international scientific management movement" (Hood 1991, 5–6).

The NPM has morphed into a variety of shapes, but the commonality to all is its call for the application of private-sector management tools and techniques to the public sector (see Barzelay 2001). It has been dissected as part of the reinventing government craze (see Osborne and Gaebler 1992) as well as the National Performance Review, the reforms to the federal government in the 1990s during Bill Clinton's administration, which underscored the glories of the "free market" (see Radin 2006).

The global revolution led to a burgeoning of NPM studies, with a host of scholars using the template to study government reforms internationally (e.g., Pollitt and Bouckaert 2004; Aucoin 1995; Zifcak 1994; Savoie 1994; Kettl 2005). Most recently some have argued that the NPM has been augmented by newer types of reforms, and indeed, that the concept itself has fallen out of fashion (Dunleavy et al. 2006). For example, Christensen and Laegreid (2007) argue that there is a "post-NPM era," whereby different contextual and structural circumstances call for more suitable types of reform, at least in an international milieu. They point out that market ideology has become institutionalized in government settings and a degree of re-regulation has occurred, thus negating the market approaches called for by early NPM precepts. In addition, they point out that the drive toward devolution as initially championed by the NPM is no longer applicable given the strengthening of the central state capacity in the countries they examine—Norway, Sweden, Denmark, Australia, and New Zealand. They and others argue that the post-NPM era calls for new reforms.

In terms of epistemological deliberations, the NPM has more or less been spared.[13] To be sure, scholars have relied upon a variety of research traditions in studying the NPM. But as Frederickson (1996, 268) points out, in the context of the reinventing movement, issues of methodology and epistemology have not been central or contested. He notes that "direct recounting of the experiences of others" has been a popular tool and "issues of replication, verification, and peer review are largely neglected."

SOCIOLOGY

Sociology has not been spared the proverbial dissection into whether it has a governing paradigm. Burrell and Morgan (1979) made a case that there is no single paradigm to govern sociological research; rather, there is a diversity of theoretical and epistemic approaches. They argue that research into organizational and sociological life can be best understood and governed by any of four paradigms of sociological inquiry: functionalist sociology, interpretive sociology, radical humanism, and radical structuralism. Functionalism and radical structuralism are based on objectivism, positivism, and nomothetic methods, and they promote a status quo view of society, whereas interpretive and radical humanism are based on subjectivism, with a nominalist ontology, antipositivist or postpositivist epistemology, and ideographic methodology; the latter two assume that social systems are conflicting and dynamic (Eriksson 2006). Although some argued that the different paradigms could lead to "disciplinary fragmentation" in sociology (Reed 1993), others have stated that they in effect illustrate the diversity of approaches for studying sociological phenomena (Hancock and Tyler 2001).

Crane and Small (1992, 198–99) argue that there is an identity crisis in sociology because, despite some commonalities within specialized clusters in the field, "from an intellectual point of view, there are few issues on which members of a discipline are unanimous. While subgroups that cross-cut various specialties will agree about the use of certain types of methods or theories, other subgroups are likely to favor alternative approaches." Moreover, like public administration, American sociology was "institutionalized 'before it had a distinctive intellectual content, a distinctive method, or even a point of view'" (Crane and Small 1992, 199, citing Oberschall 1972, 189). Crane and Small conclude that given the diversity of scope and foci in sociology, the field is not likely to gain a consensus on epistemological and methodological issues, and hence cannot achieve paradigmatic status.

It was the behavioral movement's seepage into the field of sociology that led to intellectual debates about appropriate methodologies for study. As with other social science disciplines, the question revolved around the applicability of behaviorist methods to sociology. A key proponent of creating a unified set of theoretical and methodological principles for sociology was George Homans.[14] His book *The Human Group* (1950) laid out the foundation for his later work—in particular his 1958 essay, "Social Behavior as Exchange"—where he underscored the significance of explanatory power to social phenomena, propounding that sociological research should be deductive and based on the philosophy of logical positivism.[15]

Others in the field very early on resisted a behaviorist orientation for sociology. For example, Ellwood (1930, 74) argued that "the main reasons why purely behavioristic interpretations of human society must be inadequate are: (1) they do not show the true nature of the human social process, which is essentially a process of intercommunication; (2) they do not show the true nature of adult human behavior, which is essentially cultural; and (3) they fail to show the true nature of human institutions, which are essentially based upon values and valuing processes."[16]

Kaboolian (1996, 75) points out that "sociology was founded amidst the larger debate over the nature of social phenomena and the principles governing scientific inquiry." Interestingly, her 1996 essay was a response to calls for other branches of the social sciences to assist public management in moving away from "'case-based,' 'descriptive,' and 'atheoretical'" discourse or study. She notes that sociology can contribute epistemological, ontological, and methodological insights into public management, but that sociology, like other social sciences, has "an obligation to produce knowledge of 'dual relevance' to the worlds of theory and practice" (Kaboolian 1996, 75). Thus, as she states, despite intellectual debates about epistemology and methodology in the field, "Sociology treats social 'things' as social constructions. . . . Reality is not only tangible but can be defined both objectively and subjectively. . . . The consequences of subjective reality can be real" (Kaboolian 1996, 76).

In sum, sociology, as with other social sciences, cannot claim a guiding paradigm with shared ontological, epistemological, and methodological beliefs.

EDUCATION

A number of researchers in education have questioned whether their field is governed by a paradigmatic base or has experienced paradigm shifts. For example, Patton (1990, 37) argued that a paradigm does exist, given his definition of the construct as "a world view, a general perspective, a way of breaking down the complexity of the real world. . . . Paradigms are deeply embedded in the socialization of adherents and practitioners: paradigms tell them what is important, legitimate, and reasonable. Paradigms are normative, telling the practitioner what to do without the necessity of long existential or epistemological considerations."[17]

Others changed their interpretations of an existence of a paradigm in education research over time. Lincoln and Guba, for example, in their 1985 treatise *Naturalistic Inquiry*, held that a paradigm was eminent in the field, and they continued to espouse this belief. By 2000, however, they maintained that a single paradigm in the Kuhnian sense would never emerge to govern education research (Lincoln and Guba 2000).

Looking at the issue somewhat differently, Donmoyer (2006, 11) asks whether education researchers' acceptance of qualitative methods represented a paradigm shift: "For many educational researchers working in the 1970s and early 1980s, the growing interest in and acceptance of qualitative research during that time did not represent merely the availability of new methodological options. Rather, the field's embrace of qualitative methods was seen as a sign that the field was undergoing the sort of paradigm revolution that Thomas Kuhn . . . had talked about."

Donmoyer ultimately concluded that at the time the field of education was experiencing a methodological revolution, it was appropriate to adapt the paradigmatic nomenclature advanced by Kuhn, because those who did so defined paradigm in very broad, basic terms; the "culture" at the time permitted the adaptation, according to Donmoyer. However, he argues that there can never be a paradigm because of the continued existence of a wide rift in beliefs about appropriate and relevant research traditions in the field of education. Moreover, Donmoyer (2006, 23) goes on to say that the pursuit of a paradigm "is not a viable strategy for public policy fields, including the field of education. . . . In such fields, decision-makers must consider a variety of perspectives, some of which will almost certainly be antithetical, and either find a way to balance them or choose the perspective or combination of perspectives that are appropriate for a particular situation or a particular point in time. In public policy fields, in other words, paradigm convergence is neither possible nor desirable."

PSYCHOLOGY

As with the other social sciences, psychology has also been beleaguered by questions of whether it has a paradigmatic base, and what are its appropriate methods. In a very early essay, Lipsey (1974, 406) offers this insight:

Weimer and Palermo [1973] quite rightly reject the all-too-popular pastime among psychologists of holding psychology up to the template of T. S. Kuhn's conception of scientific development and dogmatically pronouncing it paradigmatic, nonparadigmatic, or possibly pre-paradigmatic. Given a diversity of opinion, all we get from this exercise is the "yes, it is" / "no, it's not" game continued until we grow weary and disinterested. But Weimer and Palermo's rejection of template-matching occurs by way of an argument that psychology has had a paradigm (behaviourism) and a revolution (cognitive psychology), and thus is indeed paradigmatic—and we are left with the uneasy feeling that they have slipped in one final "yes, it is" while we were not looking.

By now this epistemological bantering may seem hackneyed. Yet the debates continue in the broad field of psychology (see, e.g., Staines 2008; Franco, Friedman, and Arons 2008; Borkovec and Castonguay 1998; Chambless and Hollon 1998; Weiss 1996; Binder 1996), as they do in other social sciences.[18] Lipsey (1974, 409–10) concludes with this very telling statement about the philosophy of science in the discipline of psychology: "A view from the perspective of the sociology of knowledge . . . reveals that many religious, political, social and intellectual groups are formed around shared beliefs and values. Moreover, such belief–value constellations occasionally undergo profound and even dramatic transformation. Scientists may be distinguished from other groups by the content of their shared beliefs and values and, most importantly, by their reliance on concrete problem-solutions as models for continued inquiry. Somewhere between Buddhism and biology, we find psychology. Our task is to describe its betweenness and learn what lessons we can for its future."

CONCLUSION

A seemingly clear, albeit illogical, thread seems to run through the social sciences as they question their identity, in particular the existence of a paradigmatic base. In some circles, there is derision for qualitative research as art based, metaphysical, and nonscientific. And a sloppy syllogism has emerged: Qualitative research is soft, squishy, not empirically based, and hence nonscientific. And, unfortunately, "nonscientific" ultimately translates into *nonfundable*, making it extremely challenging to secure federal or other types of funding for research in the "soft" social sciences. In fact, the divisions among political scientists over the field's scientificity has led to a congressional proposal to the National Science Foundation to cease funding for their projects. Republican senator Tom Coburn, the proposal's author, argues that the foundation should be prohibited from "wasting any federal research funding on political science projects" (Cohen 2009, C1). The celebrated political scientist Joseph Nye of the John F. Kennedy School of Government at Harvard University has argued that "'there are parts of the academy which, in the effort to be scientific, feel we should stay away from policy' because 'it interferes with science'" (Cohen 2009, C7). Nye acknowledges that the academy views quantitative research as more scientific. But as he warns, quantitative tools push political scientists "into narrow specializations, cut off from real-world concerns. The motivation . . . has overtaken the impulse to be relevant" (Cohen 2009, C7).

Good science has somehow become conflated with quantitative empiricism, in particular positivism. Thus if it is not based in logical positivism, it is pseudoscience. The constant struggles over epistemology, ontology, and methodology have culminated in a race to the bottom, which ultimately attenuates the quality and standing of any field in the social sciences.

In short public administration, like the other social sciences, has no paradigmatic base. And unlike several other branches of the social sciences, public administration is and will always be oriented toward practice, which is imbued with politics. Thus a multitude of research traditions and methodologies will always characterize the field; the relentless effort to promote science qua positivism, particularly in applied fields, only diminishes public administration's disciplinary standing in the broader arena of higher education.

NOTES

1. Also see deLeon 1997; Dryzek 1990; Danziger 1995.

2. Also see Yanow (2003), who discusses the positivist-qualitative research tradition. The political scientists at the University of California, Berkeley, perhaps best represent this view. The approach taken in this book does not correspond with this view.

3. But see Goertz (2006), who seeks to bridge the gap between qualitative and quantitative research by connecting more closely the concepts surrounding each. Also see Thomas 2008.

4. The term was elaborated upon by Lasswell and McDougal (1943). For a discussion, see Auer 2007; Fischer 1998.

5. For a discussion of the evolution of policy analysis from the standpoint of practice, see Radin (1997, 2000). As Stillman (1991, 127) points out, policy studies

began in the mid-1950s at Harvard, Berkeley, Yale, and other university departments of political science across the country. In the 1960s and early 1970s new departments and schools devoted exclusively to policy studies or analysis emerged.

6. There are others who may not classify themselves squarely in the field of policy analysis, but they have offered important alternative methods or critiques of efforts to saturate that field in a logical positivist tradition. See, e.g., Fischer 1998; Yin 2009. For early treatments, see Dror 1967; Kaplan 1986; Yanow 1987.

7. For a more detailed discussion of the history of public management and its elusive nature, see Hood 2007; Brudney, O'Toole, and Rainey 2000, 4–5.

8. See, e.g., Stivers 2000; Rainey 1990, 2003; Behn 1988, 1991, 1995, 1996; Ingraham 1995, 2007; Kettl 1993, 2005; Hood 2007. Also see, e.g., Lynn 1996; Perry 1993, 1996; Bozeman 1987, 1993; Ingraham and Romzek 1994; O'Leary 2006; O'Leary and Bingham 2009; Guy 1992, 1993.

9. As a movement, some see public management as a repudiation of the centrality of bureaucracy in executive government.

10. Conferences sponsored by the Public Management Research Association (PMRA) sought to bring together the different traditions and streams of theory around public management. Briefly, in 1991, a group of scholars from various disciplinary fields—including public management, public administration, and political science—convened a conference at the Maxwell School of Citizenship and Public Affairs at Syracuse University; it was the first National Conference on Public Management Research, out of which grew the PMRA, which holds a national conference on public management biennially. As Frederickson (1999, 1–2) points out, the conference "brought together a community of scholars with a shared interest in empirical social science research on public organizations, broadly defined, and on the development of testable theories of public policy and management." For a discussion, also see Brudney, O'Toole, and Rainey 2000.

11. See Bozeman (1993), a collection of papers presented at the first National Public Management Research Conference in 1991 in Syracuse. Its main focus was on how to study public management.

12. See Riccucci 2001.

13. But see Roberts and Bradley 1999, Ventriss 2000, and Drechsler 2005, who argue that epistemologically, the NPM is predisposed to quantification. Compare with Adams 2000 and other articles in his symposium, which address the NPM from a qualitative, postmodern perspective.

14. Also see the work of Lawrence Joseph Henderson (1935), another central figure who also supported the application of behaviorist methods to sociology. Henderson's ideas are captured by Homans (1950) in *The Human Group*.

15. Also see the work of Emerson 1972.

16. Also see Ellwood 1933; MacIver 1930.

17. Also see Shulman 1986; Erickson 1986.

18. Other examples can be seen in economics—see Medema and Samuels 2003; Ferber and Nelson 1993. However, Crane and Small (1992) argue that economics is an anomalous branch of the social sciences in that there is more consensus in the field around its epistemological and methodological bases.

Searching for Truth

THE LOGIC OF INQUIRY IN PUBLIC ADMINISTRATION

There is a chicken-and-egg conundrum in the philosophy of science about whether theory has primacy over data. Its foundation lies in the distinctions between inductive and deductive approaches to research, whereby the former moves from data or facts to theory but the latter moves from theory to data.[1] A deductive approach is concerned with testing or confirming hypotheses; it seeks to explain causal relationships between variables. It calls for the researcher's independence or objectivity and the ability to generalize findings. Conversely, inductive approaches seek to promote a greater understanding of the meanings that humans attach to events or phenomena. It presumes a degree of subjectivity on the part of the researcher and places less emphasis on the ability to generalize. It allows for changes in research approaches as the work progresses. As Miller (2008) points out, the dichotomy between induction and deduction delineates the battle lines between empiricists and the rationalists (also between the interpretivists and postmodernists). Thus Miller (2008, 14) asks: "Is knowledge generated inductively through experience or deductively from theory?"[2]

The purpose of this chapter is not to promote or glorify one approach over another but rather to illustrate the multitude of approaches that are significant for generating knowledge and ultimately for theory building and testing in public administration.[3] That is to say, the ongoing process of producing, confirming, adapting, and applying theory is not exclusive to one specific epistemic tradition. Scientific ways of knowing are based on, for example, classical theory building—which are quantitatively based, involving the development, testing, and verification of hypotheses—as well as other approaches, such as grounded theory building—which are qualitatively based, involving the collection and analysis of data and the formulation of propositions from the emergent relationships.[4]

RESEARCH APPROACHES IN
PUBLIC ADMINISTRATION

As discussed in previous chapters, if we begin with the premises that public administration has no paradigmatic base and cannot be classified as a normal science, but instead is a postnormal science, then what is the appropriate approach to research? How should scientific inquiry be carried out? By what means do we arrive at the truth in public administration or, more broadly, the social sciences? Will "scientific" methods lead us to the truth (see, e.g., Stivers 2000; Thompson 1997)? How will we know if or when we have arrived at the truth?

The field of public administration has historically generated a rich body of qualitative research, often empirically based (e.g., descriptive; best practices; case studies).[5] Even Simon, who strongly urged the field to adopt analytical tools and methods in the logical positivist tradition, contributed mainly descriptive and normative discourse to the field. Yet his work has led to a broad reliance on and acceptance of positivism in public administration.[6] Although positivism is an important approach, it is only one of many that are appropriate for postnormal sciences such as public administration. As noted in chapter 2, the postnormal sciences operate with a different level of assumptions in comparison with the normal sciences. Though the normal sciences operate under conditions marked by greater certainty and objectivity, the postnormal sciences are premised on uncertainties, values and social traditions, and anomalies. Thus a range of epistemic traditions is relevant for generating knowledge and theory building in public administration.

Table 4.1 provides a matrix comparing various approaches to research. It should be noted that there is a degree of ambiguity in the use of ontological and epistemological concepts and propositions, which emanates not only from the different branches of the social sciences but also from theological philosophies. That is to say, each discipline within the social sciences as well as the varied theologies embrace the philosophy of science in distinct or unique ways. For example, "antipositivism," a term introduced by Max Weber, was first used in the field of sociology to encourage researchers to create and use scientific methods that differed from those employed in the natural sciences. Others have equated antipositivism with deconstructionism (as conceived by Jacque Derrida), postmodernism, and/or relativism.

The matrix presented in table 4.1, although not definitive, seeks to illustrate the ontological, epistemological, and methodological bases for conducting research in the social sciences. It does not intend to promote

Table 4.1 The Philosophy of Science: Comparing Research Approaches in the Social Sciences

	Interpretivism (Antipositivism)[a]	Rationalism	Empiricism	Positivism[b]	Postpositivism	Postmodernism / Critical Theory
Ontology[d]	Relativism; knowledge and meaning are acts of interpretation; researcher and reality are inseparable, as are life and world	Researcher's mind is reality; mind comes from God	Researcher and reality are separate	Realism; researcher and reality are separate; universals exist and are real	Critical realism; researcher and reality are one and the same	Relativism; anti-realism; skepticism; collectivism; egalitarianism; pragmatism
Epistemology	Knowledge is relative; objectivity does not exist; all truth is a social construction and is culture bound	Reason is chief source of knowledge; induction; knowledge is innate; mind experience; intuition; a priori knowledge	Objective reality arises from introspective awareness, sense, and past experiences; a posteriori knowledge	Objective reality exists beyond the human mind; value neutrality; deduction	Qualified objectivity; reality exists, but is too complex to be fully understood or explained; empirical falsification	Knowledge depends on removal of ideological biases; attainment of universal truth is impossible; truth is culturally or socially constructed
Methodology	Hermeneutics; grounded theory; phenomenology; interpretation; ideographic	Inductive; speculation; commonsense reasoning; mathematical reasoning; critical reasoning	Observation; hypothesis testing; triangulation; mixed methods	Nomothetic; deductive; logically derived hypotheses; empirical testing of hypotheses; verification	Triangulation; mixed methods; modified experimental	Marxism; critical theory; radical perspectives; deconstructionism; semiotics; feminist criticism

Table 4.1 The Philosophy of Science: Comparing Research Approaches in the Social Sciences (Continued)

	Interpretivism (Antipositivism)[a]	Rationalism	Empiricism	Positivism[b]	Postpositivism[c]	Postmodernism / Critical Theory
Recording technique	Qualitative	Qualitative	Qualitative; quantitative	Quantitative	Qualitative; quantitative	Qualitative
Methods	Ethnography; action research; descriptive case studies; content and narrative analysis	Conceptual analyses; normative discourse; metaethical inquiry	Case studies; field studies; storytelling; narratives; best practices	Regression analysis (ordinary least squares; probit); structural equation modeling; experimental research	Ethnography; narratives; storytelling; case studies of Participatory Policy Analysis; Q methodology; QCA (qualitative comparative analysis)	Literary criticism; historical essays; dialectical analysis, field research; discourse analysis; case studies
Philosophers and thinkers	Goffman, Garfinkel, Schutz, Van Maanen, Silverman, Max Weber (antipositivism)	Plato, Descartes, Leibniz; Spinoza, Princess Elisabeth of Bohemia, Anne Conway	Aristotle, Epicurus, Francis Bacon, John Locke, George Berkeley, David Hume, Mary Astell,[e] Damaris Masham	Auguste Comte, Rudolf Carnap, Otto Neurath, John Stuart Mill, Herbert Spencer	Karl Popper, John Dewey, Nicholas Rescher	Jean-François Lyotard, Marx, Jacques Derrida, Michel Foucault, Nancy Scheper-Hughes, Simone de Beauvoir

[a] There is some overlap with the terms "antipositivism" and interpretivism as well as postmodernism. For a comparison of the usage of terminology, see Weber 2004, iv; and Gephart 1999.

[b] For the purposes here, positivism and logical positivism are treated alike, although strictly speaking, logical positivism combines positivism with apriorism.

[c] Postpositivism overlaps with postmodernism in that it has been used to refer to a group within political theory, mostly comprising feminists and postmodernists.

[d] Ontology generally refers to the nature of existence or being; however, it also encompasses the general features and relations of the entities that exist. It is in this latter context that ontology is used here.

[e] Mary Astell could be categorized as an empiricist in terms of her social observations, but a rationalist in terms of metaphysics.

one best way for researching matters concerning public administration but rather to generate a discussion about the utility of varied approaches to public administrative research. Some of the prominent philosophers and thinkers associated with the various approaches are also listed to encourage a further exploration of the application of philosophic thought and "science" to public administration. Examples are noted in the matrix, but chapters 5, 6, and 7 offer greater depth into the philosophic underpinnings of each approach as well as detailed examples of research within the various epistemic traditions.

As indicated in table 4.1, from an ontological standpoint, approaches to research range from positivism—where reality exists "out there" and is driven by immutable, universal, or natural laws that are completely independent of the researcher—to postmodernism, where reality is a social construction and is "in the eye of the beholder." It results from the interactions between the researcher and his or her world, and there is no single, objective truth (see, e.g., Miller 2002; Lincoln and Guba 2000; Dempster 1998; McSwite 1996, 1997; Fox and Miller 1995; Guba 1990). The ontologies are different, but no value can be ascribed to them; one is not better than the other. In fact we conduct research on the basis of *accepting* specific ontologies. For example, a postmodernist's sense of reality is governed by nominalism, whereby ideas have no objective realities but are merely names; postmodernists know a rose to be a rose because the *name* tells them it is. For positivists, however, who are grounded in realism, the reality of a concept is accepted without question and at face value. Conversely, for interpretivists, reality is strictly a matter of interpretation and for empiricists it is a function of experience.

Ontologies are ultimately based upon our *belief system* (e.g., positivists' belief that reality "is out there" or postpositivists' belief that we can never fully know). Thus as Dempster (1998) points out, even positivism, which "is generally taken to be an objective process, . . . is based on core beliefs. Such beliefs, in turn, are reinforced by understanding gained through scientific study." In short, questions of ontology inevitably rest on beliefs.

Epistemology asks "How do we know what we know?" As many have pointed out (see, e.g., Dempster 1998; Bunge 1983), epistemological questions are closely linked to ontological considerations: How can we know something without first knowing whether (or *believing*) it exists? Epistemologies, like ontologies, take many forms. That is, we know something to be true from a variety of sources. For example, we experience them in our mind (interpretivism) or empirically via our senses (touch, sight, etc.). Or we know something to be true because we feel it or have been told it by a credible source (see Fernández-Armesto 1997). For postpositivists, truth or knowledge is not bedrock but is conjectural. According to the eminent political and social philosopher Karl Popper (1963, 1977), human knowledge could only be gained through empirical falsification (see Fischer 1998). Falsification is a process of "conjectures and refutations." Hypotheses, propositions, or theories cannot be scientific unless there is the possibility of a contrary case. The process of accumulating knowledge involves formulating hypotheses and then trying to prove them wrong. In this sense, hypotheses can never be proven correct because of the possibility that one or more experiments could prove them wrong. Thus we can approximate, but never fully know, reality.

For logical positivists, conversely, there is no room for metaphysical speculation, reason, or innate ideas, as called for by the rationalists. Truth and knowledge are gained through deduction and explanatory designs. Positivists maintain that logical and mathematical propositions are tautological and that moral and value statements are merely emotive. The goal of knowledge, according to this approach, is to describe the phenomena experienced (Riccucci 2006). It should further be noted that positivism values both "pure" and "applied" research. Although public administration is an applied field, positivists would argue that both applied research —which seeks to apply knowledge and truths—and pure or basic research—whereby knowledge is sought without concern for application— can be pursued.

Methodology, or the theory and analysis of how research should proceed, is equally linked with ontologies and epistemologies. Indeed, methodology and hence choice of method, or the procedure for gathering evidence and even recording technique, depend upon our ontological and epistemological frameworks.[8] So conducting research in any of the social sciences involves not simply making choices about methodology; it hinges on the researcher's ontological and epistemological suppositions. Bunge (1983, xiv) points out that "methodology . . . is the discipline that studies the principles of successful inquiry, whether in ordinary life, science, technology or the humanities. . . . It is descriptive and analytical, but in addition it is prescriptive or normative: it attempts to find out not only how people actually get to know but also how they ought to proceed in order to attain their cognitive goals."

The research methods as well as recording techniques given in table 4.1 represent some examples. These categories are not discrete; so, for example, content analysis, although ascribed to interpretivism, can be employed in other approaches, as can case studies.[9]

For positivists, study must be nomothetic (i.e., searching for abstract universal principles or laws); deductive; and based on value-free, rationally derived, testable, and *verifiable* hypotheses. They maintain that "questions answerable through natural science methods of testing and confirmation are the *only* legitimately answerable questions, and the correct answers can only come from those methods" (Little 2000, 5; emphasis in the original). Interpretivists, conversely, subscribe to hermeneutics (i.e., using textual analysis to discern reality) and phenomenology (i.e., conceptualizing phenomena through acts of consciousness), whereby qualitative case studies and best practices research are valued. For empiricists, observation is key, and it can be expressed through, for example, storytelling or narratives. Postpositivists emphasize the importance of triangulation, multiple measures, and observations, each of which may possess different types of error; ultimately, multiple realities manifest simultaneously (Lincoln and Guba 2000; Guba 1990). Through an increased reliance on mixed methods, postpositivist methodology seeks to falsify rather than verify hypotheses.

In sum, there are various ontological, epistemological, and methodological bases for conducting research in any of the social sciences. And regardless of the approach, choice and subjectivity are invariably present. As Dempster (1998) points out, the challenge is "recogniz[ing] the gray areas that exist among and between [the various approaches to conducting research]. . . . Tailoring research approaches to match characteristics of particular situations is not only valuable, but essential. . . . Plural perspectives offer the potential for strong contributions to research."

AN ILLUSTRATION: RESEARCH ON REPRESENTATIVE BUREAUCRACY

Chapters 5, 6, and 7 provide several examples of studies in the various epistemic traditions. But here, table 4.2 superimposes the template set forth in table 4.1 to provide examples of studies in one area—representative bureaucracy—to illustrate the use of the various epistemic traditions and methodologies in public administration research. Because these examples are only illustrative, there is overlap between and among them.

Representative bureaucracy is a normative theory that calls for bureaucracy's social composition to reflect that of the general population. The term "representative bureaucracy," coined by Kingsley in 1944, supposes that bureaucratic legitimacy is augmented and strengthened when bureaucracy is representative of the population it serves. As seen in table 4.2, one

Table 4.2 A Comparison of Research Approaches to Studies of Representative Bureaucracy

Interpretivism (Antipositivism)	Rationalism	Empiricism	Positivism	Postpositivism	Postmodernism/ Critical Theory
Legal studies on affirmative action, the primary means for achieving representative bureaucracies; case studies on hiring and promotion practices	Studies where the attainment of knowledge about representative bureaucracy is based upon reasoning, not experience or sense perception	Research pointing to evidence, attained through the senses, of the existence of representative bureaucracy	Research empirically testing and verifying the existence of a link between passive and active representation	Research examining the existence of representative bureaucracy through mixed methods	Research challenging the mainstream tenets and suppositions of representative bureaucracy as the chief tool for achieving multiculturalism
Example: Kellough 2006	Example: Mosher 1968	Example: Cayer and Sigelman 1980	Example: Meier, Wrinkle, and Polinard 1999	Example: Naff 2001	Example: Hutchinson and Mann 2004
Exhaustive review of statutory, constitutional, and case law governing affirmative action programs and policies	Provides reasoning for the various conceptions of representative bureaucracy (e.g., passive and active)	Provides descriptive statistics on the existence of passive representativeness overall in state and local government jobs, and by job level or function	Regression results indicate that students of color as well as white students benefit from representative bureaucracy at the street level	Through the use of qualitative and quantitative methods, illustrates the degree to which the federal government has achieved representativeness, and the various barriers that prevent representativeness	Fosters acceptance of diversity in ontologies and methodologies in order to deconstruct male hegemony and promote nongendered organizational structures

example of the interpretive approach to representative bureaucracy can be seen in any of the multitude of studies examining the law as it pertains to affirmative action, perhaps the most important tool for achieving representative bureaucracy and more broadly diversity in the workplace. Kellough's (2006) book *Understanding Affirmative Action* serves as an example here. He begins with a review of the historical developments of affirmative action, including an in-depth examination of the statutory and constitutional law governing employment discrimination and affirmative action. He then provides an extensive review of the case law, or court rulings on affirmative action, carefully illustrating how the U.S. Constitution and statutes such as Title VII of the Civil Rights Act of 1964 as amended create parameters for the legal operation of affirmative action policies and programs.

Kellough (2006, 80) stresses the importance of affirmative action for representative bureaucracy. He argues that "when the public workforce is more representative of the people served, its diversity will help to ensure that all interests are represented in bureaucratic policy making." He goes on to say that the "concept of representative bureaucracy is salient because substantial power to shape or establish public policy rests in the hands of government employees."

A rationalist perspective on representative bureaucracy can be found in Mosher's 1968 classic, *Democracy and the Public Service.* He addresses not only the history of public service and the importance of merit and professionalism to public service but also the topic of social equity in the context of representative bureaucracy. He explicates the concept as devised by Kingsley (1944), reasoning that the concept of representativeness should be bifurcated into passive and active representation. Passive representation, he proposes, exists when the social characteristics of a bureaucracy perfectly mirror that of the general population. If a city's population includes, let us say, 8 percent African Americans, then the city's bureaucracy ought to also include 8 percent African Americans. Active representativeness, he maintains, goes even further to state that legitimate or true representation of the city's African Americans will occur only to the extent that they fill positions in the city bureaucracy whereby they can push for the values and interests of their counterparts in the city's general population. Active representation presumes that the social characteristics of an individual will predict his or her behaviors and actions.

An example of representative bureaucracy in the tradition of empiricism can be seen in Cayer and Sigelman's (1980) descriptive examination of the representativeness of women and people of color in state and local government for 1973 and 1975. They constructed a representativeness ratio, which divided the percentage of the group in the government work-force by their percentage in the general population, and Cayer and Sigel-man (1980, 445) noted that "a ratio of 1.0 means that group occupied the same proportion of government jobs that it did of the general population; a lower ratio signifies numerical underrepresentation, and a higher ratio overrepresentation."

Cayer and Sigelman found that for the two periods studied, white men were overrepresented in state and local government jobs, whereas women and people of color (with the exception of Asian Americans) were under-represented. They further found that women and people of color were more represented in those jobs or functions traditionally or historically filled by those groups, such as public welfare, hospitals, housing, and health; they were grossly underrepresented, however, in functions such as police and firefighting.

Kenneth Meier has considerably advanced our knowledge and under-standing of representative bureaucracy from the perspective of positivism. One of his myriad studies, for example, relied on a pooled time-series analysis of 350 school districts with at least 1,000 students from Texas between 1991 and 1996 to determine whether representative bureaucracy produced gains for students of color at the expense of whites (Meier, Wrinkle, and Polinard 1999). The pooled data for this study resulted in more than 2,000 usable cases. The dependent variable was student perform-ance, as measured by students' pass rates on annual standardized tests in grades 3, 5, 8, and 10. The primary independent variable was the percentage of Latino and African American teachers. Other independent or control variables—factors other than race that can influence educational perform-ance—included (1) poverty, as measured by the percentage of students who qualify for free or reduced-price meals; (2) school expenditures, as measured by the percentage of state funding received, average teacher salary, and cost of instruction per pupil; (3) environmental factors such as class size—as measured by the student/teacher ratio—and the number of students enrolled in gifted classes; and (4) teacher experience, as measured by the average years of service. One other factor that could determine student performance is the innate abilities of students, for which the authors were unable to control.

Through regression analyses, Meier, Wrinkle, and Polinard (1999, 1036) found that "moving toward a more representative bureaucracy will not have outcomes detrimental to the established majority. Instead of minority students' gains coming at the expense of Anglo students, both groups benefit from higher levels of minority representation of street-level bureau-crats—teachers—in the education system. There appear to be no redistri-butional consequences." On the basis of their findings, they offered the following "provocative new hypothesis for organizational studies: *Repre-sentative bureaucracies are more effective at meeting their goals than nonrep-resentative bureaucracies in similar circumstances*" (Meier, Wrinkle, and Polinard 1999, 1037; emphasis in the original). They go on to say that the "underlying logic of this hypothesis rests on the notion that discriminatory personnel policies result in less able employees, which, in turn, detrimen-tally affects agency performance. Representative bureaucracies do not erect such artificial barriers to organizational performance and thus will perform at a higher level than those with discriminatory hiring practices" (Meier, Wrinkle, and Polinard 1999, 1037).

An example of research on representative bureaucracy in the postposi-tivist tradition can be seen in Naff's (2001) book *To Look Like America: Dismantling Barriers for Women and Minorities in Government*. Naff relies on mixed methods to determine not only the degree to which the federal government is representative of women and people of color but also whether they are afforded the same opportunities and positions of powers as white men. She provides a careful analysis of the court rulings on affirmative action, descriptive data on the percentages of women and peo-ple of color in the federal government, and regression results for factors that could affect their advancement.

Naff's chapter on the glass ceiling provides an excellent historical discus-sion of this concept, which refers to the artificial barriers that prevent women from reaching higher-level positions. Here she provides not only a host of descriptive statistics and regression results but also comments from focus group participants, which expound upon the quantitative find-ings. For example, one of the factors deemed significant as a result of regression analysis is the impact of the number of hours workers devote to their jobs each week. To provide a more in-depth explanation of this factor, Naff presents a series of responses by focus group participants such as the following:

♦ In my division [the boss] would come through and he would say, "I expect to see all your faces when I come here in the morning, and I expect to see you here when I leave at night. And only the people who do that will be promoted."

♦ . . . And I have worked in organizations . . . where the leadership tended to be there until 6:30, 7:00, 7:30 in the evening. And to the extent that you wanted to become part of the management team, you didn't leave at 5:30. You simply didn't.

♦ I think that there's the ethic in this department, if you're in the [Senior Executive Service], you really better be available from seven to seven. It's strong in some places. (Naff 2001, 78)

Through the use of mixed methods, Naff provides a full picture of the degree to which representative bureaucracy exists, some of the barriers to fully achieving such a bureaucracy (e.g., inconsistent leadership and the inadequacy of the equal employment opportunity grievance process), and recommendations for how the federal government can surmount these and other barriers.

Postmodernists address the topic of representative bureaucracy from the standpoint of critical theory. They reject the narrow conception of representative bureaucracy as a means for achieving diversity or multiculturalism. Box (2007, 163) summarizes their position in this fashion: "Representative bureaucracy is public administration's response to the civil rights movement. While it was certainly a move forward, it has not produced the form of cultural pluralism or relativism that would be associated with multiculturalism. The trouble with the field of public administration is that it has not properly engaged the issue of multiculturalism from perspectives other than passive or active representation of groups or group interests."

Hutchinson and Mann's (2004, 79) research addresses this concern with respect to gender. They argue that the research in public administration "continues in a narrow conceptual framework that leaves many frustrated and wondering if real change for women will ever be fully realized." Part of the problem, they maintain, is that there is no "defining body of feminist theory in our field." They offer strategies for promoting feminism in public administration. First they argue that traditional feminist theories do not go far enough in efforts to advance feminist ways of thinking and doing in public administration. That is, traditional affirmative action programs and pay equity strategies, for example, though important, seek to create equality for women in a male-dominated world. They state that incorporating women into the preexisting bureaucratic structures will not resolve the problem, because those organizational structures and cultures are constructed and conceptualized by men. Rather, changes are in order not in the structures themselves but in the manner in which they are viewed—indeed conceptualized. Hutchinson and Mann (2004, 81) call for a deconstruction and reexamination of "the fundamental theories, mechanisms of analysis and primary values that have given shape to our epistemological techniques and our ontological assumptions generally, and in public administration in particular. Sought here is a fundamental shift in human knowledge that results from 'seeing' through the feminist lens. For us, this shift necessitates the recognition that we truly are living in a 'man's world,' and since we'd rather not, we are obliged to employ a non-masculinist approach to epistemology and methodology and in the process remake ourselves in our own image." They conclude that this "add women and stir" formula will not lead to substantive change in the gender images of public administration.

Hutchinson and Mann then argue that radical/cultural feminism goes too far. This brand of feminist theory holds that the chief source of women's power is not in the office or position they hold in society but rather in their reproductive capabilities. Hutchinson and Mann (2004, 83) argue that the "radical feminist stance seems of little importance to the field of public administration, except that the in-your-face quality of the discourse is the jolt that is often needed to move our thinking forward to each successive, new level of insight."

Hutchinson and Mann (2004, 83) instead propose a postmodern feminism "which focuses on the value of difference, argues that the search for one, common feminist standpoint or 'reality' is not only futile but just another example of how male language and culture attempts to erase the valuable differences which exist among women, as well as women and men." They argue for the deconstruction of male hegemony in order to promote nongendered organizational structures. One way to accomplish this is to encourage the public administration community to at least begin to acknowledge that there are a multitude of approaches to ways of thinking, knowing, and doing—and that public administration thus needs to support a diversity of ontologies, epistemologies, and methodologies. They, suggest for example, that public administrationists consider "that sex and gender are one and at the same time, multiple, and that culture is not only broadly geographical in the traditional sense, it encompasses the 'geography' of humanness. . . . By accepting our multiple permutations, we do two things: we acknowledge the devastating consequences of defining each other using the narrow constructs of outward appearances and correct them, and by doing so, we liberate one another to achieve the full range of opportunities for self-actualization—for women, *and men*" (Hutchinson and Mann 2004, 91–92; emphasis in the original).

Hutchinson and Mann (2004, 80) stress that the regendering of public administration will take time. They state: "We submit that a project of this magnitude, a feminist re-visioning of public administration . . . is the work of generations and one we are beginning none too soon."

In sum, representative bureaucracy lends itself to research within a number of different epistemic traditions. One is not better than or preferred to another; rather, each advances our body of knowledge in different ways with respect to this significant area of study in public administration.

STRENGTHS AND LIMITATIONS OF THE VARIOUS EPISTEMIC TRADITIONS

The question of the strengths and limitations of qualitative and quantitative research approaches is perhaps at the core of the dissension among public administrationists as to what methods are most appropriate for theory building in the field. Certainly there are arguments for and against both qualitative and quantitative methods that can be found in any introductory book on research methods. For example, as Elman (2008) points out, qualitative research has inferential problems, whereby quantitative research does not. Conversely, quantitative research, unlike qualitative research, suffers from potential problems rising from case selection and degrees of freedom. But as stressed throughout this book, there can be no agreement about the pros and cons of either because of the conflicting underlying philosophies of knowledge associated with each. In addition, the premise of this book is that all research traditions add value to public administration; the relevancy of qualitative or quantitative tools depends on the research question and the underlying epistemologies and ontologies. As Maxwell (2005, 22–23; emphasis in the original) argues: "Qualitative and quantitative methods are not simply different ways of doing the same thing. Instead, they have different strengths and logics, and are often best used to address different kinds of questions and goals. . . . Quantitative researchers tend to be interested in whether and to what extent *variance* in *x* causes variance in *y*. Qualitative researchers, on the other hand, tend to ask *how* *x* plays a role in causing *y*, what the *process* is that connects *x* and *y*."

Gerring and Thomas (2005) argue that the division between quantitative and qualitative research designs can be best understood through the concept of comparability. They

> present a new way of thinking about these issues that rests upon the key concept of *comparability*. At the level of observations, we argue . . . that the principal factor separating qualitative observations from quantitative observations is the relative comparability of evidence. Quantitative observations presume a population of things that can be readily measured, counted,

and hence compared. Qualitative observations, by contrast, presume an empirical field where individual pieces of evidence are not directly comparable to one another, at least not to the extent that they can be precisely measured. . . . The key point is that the difference between these two kinds of observations rests on the presumed comparability of adjacent observations, not (at least not directly) on the size of N, the style of presentation (numbers or narrative), epistemology, ontology, or the formal structure of the method. (Gerring and Thomas 2005, 2; emphasis in the original)

To avoid the dystopic tug of war that invariably results from a comparison of the various approaches, a laundry list of the strengths and limitations of each is not presented; such discussions, as noted, can be found elsewhere. Moreover, the presentation and discussion of the various epistemic traditions presented above (also see table 4.1 and chapters 5, 6, and 7) obliquely point to the comparative strengths and limitations of each. For example, most qualitative approaches reject that there can be a value-free science and an objective external reality. However, these factors represent the very essence—the underlying principles or tenets—of logical positivism. Another example can be seen in critical realism, which holds that all measurement is fallible. To logical positivists, therefore, the fundamental nature of critical realism is a limitation. May and Mumby (2005, 31) make this observation: Qualitative approaches such as interpretivism "assume that subjective understandings have a key impact on scientific process . . . [and] that objectivity is an emergent collective interpretation rather than an inherent property of a particular observational act." The point here is that the strengths of one approach may be considered limitations from the perspective of other approaches precisely because of the underlying ontologies and epistemologies associated with each.

The same can be said for the concepts of validity and reliability, which are important for any research tradition but represent a major chasm between logical positivists and all other philosophies of science.[10] There are different types of validity (e.g., construct, internal, external), but in general it refers to the strength of research propositions or conclusions, or, more traditionally, the extent to which a test measures what it claims to measure. Reliability refers to the consistency of measurement and the replicability of findings. Logical positivists view these concepts as a fundamental benchmark for sound scientific research. Others argue that because validity and reliability are constructs, developed in the natural sciences, their applicability to qualitative research is more tenuous because of the manner in which these concepts have been construed by positivists. Thus the fundamental differences in the nature of qualitative and quantitative research defy a standard application of validity and reliability to research. Ritchie and Lewis (2003, 270), for example, point out that "tests or measures of reliability and validity, as used in mathematical or physical sciences, are wholly inappropriate for qualitative investigation and cause considerable confusion when applied. But in their broadest conception, reliability meaning 'sustainable' and validity meaning 'well grounded' will have relevance for qualitative research since they help to define the strength of the data. This is of particular concern in the context of generalisation where the ability to transfer findings to other contexts or wider theory will be circumscribed by the soundness of the evidence."

Yanow and Schwartz-Shea (2006b, xvii; emphasis in the original) approach the matter similarly. They state that efforts to "improve the quality (from the point of view of methodological positivism) of meaning-focused studies have brought them under pressure to conform to the validity and reliability criteria that characterize quantitative methods and methodologies. What is problematic here is that quantitative methods are, by and large, informed by positivist philosophical presuppositions, *and their evaluative criteria have grown out of these ontological and epistemological presuppositions*, whereas traditional qualitative methods are informed, explicitly or not, by interpretive philosophical presuppositions and have their own evaluative measures."

In short, the underlying values and assumptions of the various epistemic traditions drive the relevance of validity and reliability. As has been noted, reliability generally refers to the replicability of research. But if interpretivists and postmodernists cannot conceive of a single reality, replication has no significance or relevance. Similarly, the concept of validity, whether internal or external, assumes unique connotations for qualitative research. As Ritchie and Lewis (2003, 273) point out, the questions posed in qualitative research "are different ones and relate more to the validity of representation, understanding and interpretation."

Table 4.3 provides a comparative view of how validity, reliability, and generalizability have been conceptualized from the perspective of qualitative and quantitative research. A more universal view is also presented. Again, it is recognized that these concepts are schismatic, representing perhaps the sine qua non for the antagonism between the logical positivist and nonpositivist research traditions; but they are offered here to illustrate how each research tradition justifies its basis for advancing knowledge and truth in public administration.

Table 4.3 A Comparative View of Validity, Reliability, and Generalizability

Criterion	Terminology in Logical Positivism	Terminology in Other Research Traditions	Universal Terms
Truth value	Internal validity	Credibility	Authenticity
Applicability	External validity / generalizability	Transferability	Fittingness
Consistency	Reliability	Dependability	Auditability
Neutrality	Objectivity	Conformability	Utilization/application/ action

Sources: Schwartz-Shea 2006, 94; Lincoln and Guba 1985; Miles and Huberman 1994.

There is one approach to research—triangulation, or mixed methods— that perhaps bridges the gaping cleavage between qualitative and quantitative approaches, drawing on the strengths of each.[11] In general triangulation is the intentional use of mixed methods, especially to offset the shortcomings in each method individually and to strengthen the validity and reliability of study findings. Although we generally think of triangulation in terms of relying on both quantitative and qualitative methods, as empiricists and postpositivists sometimes do, triangulation has also been relied upon *within* qualitative and quantitative traditions. Moreover, triangulation can be used in the context of data, theory, methodology, the unit of analysis, and even the investigator (see Lee 2006b).

It should further be noted that the concepts of triangulation and mixed methods are often used interchangeably (see, e.g., Creswell 2009). Others, however, view them separately. For example, Kadushin and colleagues (2008, 46) state: "Triangulation is used to describe 'severe' statistical tests of correlation between alternative quantitative measurements and is employed to test the accuracy of those measurements. In contrast, the broader concept of mixed methods describes the integration of diverse qualitative and quantitative approaches and is employed to build theory." Such a distinction is not drawn here.

Creswell (2009, 14) notes that the "concept of mixing different methods originated in 1959 when Campbell and Fisk used multimethods to study validity of psychological traits." This led to the use of mixed methods, combining qualitative and quantitative tools. Creswell goes on to say that mixed methods serve to balance out the shortcomings and strengths of both qualitative and quantitative methods: "Recognizing that all methods have limitations, researchers felt that biases inherent in any single method could neutralize or cancel the biases of other methods. Triangulating data sources—a means for seeking convergence across qualitative and quantitative methods—was born" (Creswell 2009, 14). Chapter 7 provides examples of research in public administration that employs mixed methods.

DISCUSSION

As in other social sciences, theory building in public administration has been overshadowed by questions about methodology. In particular there continues to be a wholesale dismissal of qualitative research as not contributing to theory building (see Gerring and Thomas 2005). Stivers (2000) observes that some within the field of public administration continue to struggle in vain to make public administration more "scientific," through the application of quantitatively based empirical research (also see McCurdy and Cleary 1984; White 1999). But as argued here, the contextual issues and variables that surround the research question, along with *the underlying assumptions that researchers make about ontology and epistemology*, determine the suitability of the analytical tools.

Adams and White (1994) argue that method or technique sometimes overshadows other important considerations for research in public administration (also see Box 1992; White and Adams 1994a, 1994b). They point out that "when technique alone assumes paramount importance, it is an easy . . . next step to omit a framework, or fail to address theory-building, among other pitfalls. Technique may even dictate the choice of topic (e.g., what problem can statistic X be applied to). One cannot help but wonder whether courses on research methods, often taught as 'toolkits' and divorced from the substantive content of the field, have fostered . . . mindless empiricism" (Adams and White 1994, 573).

Adams and White (1994, 574) conclude that the lure of "technique can replace theoretical reflection. . . . A fascination with technique and its use essentially drives out the larger substantive concerns within which the research problem is embedded." This proclivity, they argue, ultimately leads to a "theoretical wasteland" in public administration.

As argued here, the logic of inquiry in the field of public administration is multifaceted. As with any postnormal science, there is immense room for diversity in research traditions. The important point is that as a social science, public administration continues to advance as a field of inquiry. Progress is made with each piece of good, sound research, notwithstanding the methodology.[12] The next three chapters present examples of the use of the various research traditions in public administration. The goal is to point to examples of scholarship in the various epistemic traditions that have contributed to theory building so that others can further develop theory, test theory, or even glean ideas for strengthening research in public administration. Ultimately, the community of scholars in the field can potentially speak with one another instead of at or around each other.

NOTES

1. This chapter does not pit deductive versus inductive theory building against one another. The dichotomy between deductive and inductive approaches has only served as a cleavage to judge the importance or significance of research in public administration.

2. Also see McCurdy and Cleary 1984; White 1986, 1992, 1999; Perry 1991; Perry and Kraemer 1986, 1990; Hummel 1991; and Adams 1992.

3. Some have argued that theory building is not the sole goal of research, particularly in applied fields. See Bowman 2008, 97. Some maintain that qualitative methods tend to be more appropriate in the early stages of research and for theory building and that quantitative methods are more appropriate when theory is well developed, and for purposes of theory testing and refinement. No such distinctions are made here. See Kenworthy 2008.

4. Other qualitatively based approaches include modeling, narrative analysis, discourse analysis, and hermeneutics, as noted in table 4.1. Others will also be addressed in chapter 5. Also see Yanow 2009; Yanow and Schwartz-Shea 2006a; McNabb 2008.

5. Some have charged early research in public administration as being atheoretical, but this reflects a narrow conception of theory. Early research in public administration has contributed immensely to theory building in the field. For a discussion, see, e.g., Bertelli and Lynn 2006.

6. Positivism and logical positivism are treated interchangeably here. Also, it is important to note that although some claim that as a movement it is dead (see, e.g., Meier 2005), its legacy in the field of public administration as a philosophy of science continues, and therefore the classification is applied in this treatise.

7. I use the term "realism" as distinct from critical realism or other conceptions of realism (e.g., scientific realism, commonsense philosophical realism). Realism in the context here assumes that a thought- or mind-independent reality exists. Critical realism asserts that there is a reality "out there" but that our knowledge will always be limited and mutable because it is made up of the world, our perception of it, and us. For different and overlapping treatments of these concepts, see, e.g., Little 2000; Sayer 2000; Niiniluoto 1999; Leplin 1984; Feyerabend 1981.

8. Method and methodology are sometimes used interchangeably. They are not here. For a discussion see, e.g., Crotty 1998; Dempster 1998; Guba 1990; Harding 1987; Bunge 1983.

9. See Fuchs and Sandoval 2008, who analyze text by the method of quantifying qualitative content analysis.

10. The significance of validity and reliability to quantitative research has been addressed extensively in textbooks. Their importance to qualitative research has also been addressed (see Creswell 2009; Ritchie and Lewis 2003; Amaratunga and Baldry 2001; Healy and Perry 2000; and Kelle and Laurie 1995), particularly in the context of case studies (see Yin 2009; McNabb 2008; Dul and Hak 2008; and Agranoff and Radin 1991).

11. For a discussion of the link between mixed methods and pragmatism as a philosophical position, see, e.g., Tashakkori and Teddlie 2003.

12. Of course, disagreement certainly arises over what constitutes good, sound research.

Theory Building through Qualitative Approaches

This chapter examines contributions to the generation of knowledge and theory building in public administration that have relied on qualitative approaches. As emphasized throughout this book, the perspective taken here is that all research—whether positivist or interpretivist, qualitative or quantitative—can potentially contribute to theory building in the field.[1] Individually and collectively, public administration research can provide additive value to the theory-building cycle.

Certainly there is an array of treatises addressing qualitative methods in the social sciences (see, e.g., Yang and Miller 2008; Yin 2009; McNabb 2008; Yanow and Schwartz-Shea 2006a; Creswell 2006; Denzin and Lincoln 2005; Ritchie and Lewis 2003; White 1999; Miles and Huberman 1994). This chapter is not an introductory "how-to" or "nuts and bolts" discourse on qualitative research methods. Instead it examines the various qualitative epistemic traditions in the social sciences—as presented in table 4.1 of the previous chapter—and how public administration and management scholars have employed them. Particular emphasis is given to the use of research methods in the field. The net is cast widely to include books as well as studies from a number of journals on public administration and management.

The research approaches discussed here, as presented in the previous chapter, include interpretivism, rationalism, empiricism, postpositivism, and postmodernism. As noted in chapter 4, there is a degree of overlap between and among the various epistemic traditions (e.g., interpretivism with postmodernism), and so the categories are not discrete.[2] But the purpose here is not to pigeonhole examples of research into preconceived boxes but rather to provide illustrations of the various uses of the epistemic approaches.

INTERPRETIVISM

As noted in chapter 4, interpretivism represents a philosophic tradition based on the interpretive nature of knowledge. The knowledge built by interpretivists or constructionists is based on their own worldviews, history, culture, and experiences, and how they interpret the worldviews and ideas of the people they are studying.[3] Moreover, knowledge does not exist independently of consciousness. For interpretivists knowledge is a culturally bound social construction. As Crotty (1998, 67; emphasis in the original) points out: "Interpretivism is often linked to the thought of Max Weber, . . . who suggests that in the human sciences we are concerned with *Verstehen* (understanding). This has been taken to mean that Weber is contrasting the interpretive approach (*Verstehen*, understanding) needed in human and social sciences with the explicative approach (*Erklären*, explaining), focused on causality, that is found in the natural sciences."

Yanow and Schwartz-Shea (2006b, xi) point out that "researchers in all sciences—natural, physical, and human or social—interpret their data. Moreover, the interpretive processes for analyzing texts in what might be called literary social science, such as what is done by historians, political theorists (or political philosophers), and feminist theorists, overlap with those used, for example, in analyzing contemporary governmental or organizational documents."[4]

Public administration scholars who examine government texts and related documents (e.g., court rulings, the U.S. Constitution) are one example of the interpretivist approach with a reliance on, for instance, hermeneutics. Hermeneutics entails textual interpretation or analysis to discover the meaning behind the written word.[5] Because of the significance of language, history, and social and cultural milieus in hermeneutics, interpretations cannot be devoid of values. An example of interpretivism with a reliance on hermeneutics can be seen in examinations of the U.S. Constitution from the perspective of the Framers and their intent of the document's Preamble and each of its original seven articles. So, too, would be an interpretation of the justification for the Bill of Rights and the other amendments to the U.S. Constitution. An examination of court rulings, whereby judges or justices interpret the Framers' intent in order to craft their decisions or rulings, is another example.

A number of scholars have examined various facets of the U.S. Constitution from these perspectives, most notably David Rosenbloom. In several studies, including one of his earliest books, *Federal Service and the Constitution*, Rosenbloom (1971) examined the contextual meaning of the U.S. Constitution with respect to the employment rights of federal workers.[6]

He draws on early interpretations of government employment as a type of property from which an individual could not be separated without cause. He contrasts this with later interpretations of government office as a form of privilege with no constitutional protections. He unravels in great detail the doctrine of privilege, in particular judicial construal of that doctrine in light of the original intent of the Framers. He shows that the ensuing court decisions—often very narrow—have set parameters for the meaning and connotations of employment rights in government. His work on these subjects has contributed immensely to theory building in the areas of judicial interpretation of the U.S. Constitution and ensuing decision making by the courts.

John Rohr's 1986 classic *To Run a Constitution: The Legitimacy of the Administrative State* is also representative of research in the interpretivist tradition that has contributed greatly to theory building in public administration. Rohr takes the debates of the nation's Founders into a more contemporary context in his defense of the administrative state. Drawing on the U.S. Constitution and the Federalist Papers, Rohr illustrates that the administrative state was not in fact extraneous or contrary to original intent, but rather representative of the Founders' moral intentions for governing the nation. He argues that public administrators are "constitutional masters" who have a moral as well as technical responsibility to promote the public will. Like Rosenbloom, he sees the U.S. Constitution as a primary pillar of American public administration. Rohr's work here adds significantly to constitutional scholarship and theory in the field.[7]

A number of other scholars have written on judicial, legal, and administrative decision making and rulemaking in the same interpretivist tradition, generally relying on hermeneutics. The works of Cooper (1988, 1999, 2002a, 2002b), O'Leary (2006), Carroll (1987), Roberts (1988, 2007), and West (1985, 2005), for example, have further advanced our knowledge in these critical areas of public administrative theory.

Interpretivists also rely on case studies, as seen, for example, in Craig Thomas's 2003 book, *Bureaucratic Landscapes: Interagency Cooperation and the Preservation of Biodiversity.*[8] Through case studies, Thomas examines California's interagency cooperative efforts to preserve biodiversity—that is, the diversity of species, ecosystems, and habitats. In particular, he examines the motivations of government officials to cooperate with one another. As Thomas (2003, xiv) points out, "I slice the agencies into three cross sections, representing line managers, professional staff, and field staff, and demonstrate how these individuals understand the world in fundamentally different ways." He asks how the diverging values of various types of officials—line managers (desire for autonomy), professional staff (specialists, concerned with advancing their field or profession), and field staff (desire to interact with the local community)—lead to interagency cooperation. He finds that these officials cooperate when there is some form of interdependence. A key factor leading to interdependence is lawsuits filed by environmental activists under, among other laws, the Endangered Species Act. He finds that the threat of lawsuits and possible court orders conditions the motivations of the various types of officials, thus leading to interagency cooperation.

Content analysis represents another qualitative method sometimes employed by interpretivists. Content analysis examines text or speech to discover what if any themes emerge and how the themes interrelate. Babbie (2006) defines content analysis as the study of recorded human communications. An example in the social sciences can be seen in any of the vast amount of research, which analyzes various forms of text or recorded transcripts of participant interviews. For example, Radin relies on content analysis in her 2006 book *Challenging the Performance Movement: Accountability, Complexity, and Democratic Values*, which further pulls and pushes the performance management literature in considerably new and innovative directions. Radin spent more than a decade analyzing the Government Performance and Results Act (GPRA) and, more recently, the Program Assessment Rating Tool, known as PART. In fact, she was extremely close to the GPRA process in that she served under Donna Shalala at the U.S. Department of Health and Human Services during the early stages of GPRA's implementation.

Through the use of fictitious characters grappling with implementation dilemmas, Radin makes the persuasive case that the performance movement clashes with the realpolitik of government operations, thereby rendering it counterproductive. Given its private-sector underpinnings, she argues that the public administration community must move beyond the conventional one-size-fits-all solutions to performance measurement, which diminish professionalism and, paradoxically, organizational performance. She fills a major gap in the performance literature by offering an alternative approach to the generic, one-best-way approach to performance management and measurement: the "program approach," which accounts for the complex set of actors within a highly politicized environment. The program approach is bottom up rather than top down, as prescribed by the generic approach; it supports multiple values rather than efficiency and effectiveness as prescribed by the generic approach. Compliance is tied to specific programs rather than government-wide programs, and management is seen as a means to program ends, rather than as a separate, distinct activity, divorced from specific programs. Her research contributes greatly to public administrative theory in the context of performance management and more broadly public management.

Another example of interpretivists' use of content analysis of recorded transcripts of participant interviews can be seen in the work of Melitski (2003), who relies on content analysis of interview transcripts in his examination of the types of information technology initiatives and investments of public agencies in their efforts to enhance the performance capabilities of their e-government endeavors.[9] His research here has contributed to the body of knowledge in the areas of performance management and e-governance.

Other examples of content analysis in the interpretivist tradition can be seen in any of the vast number of examinations of case law concerned with administrative matters.[10] For example, Rosemary O'Leary's (1995) *Environmental Change: Federal Courts and the EPA* examines the impact of federal court decisions on the policies and managerial practices of the Environmental Protection Agency (EPA) in every statutory area: clean air, clean water, hazardous waste cleanup, controlled pesticide use, resource conservation and recovery, safe drinking water, and the control of toxic substances. She analyzed the content of more than 2,000 federal court decisions in addition to archival material and agency memos to demonstrate the cumulative effect of judges' decisions to regulate the behavior of the EPA and ultimately environmental policy in the aforementioned areas. Her research illustrates the intricacies of the judicial administrative relationship and shows that, contrary to existing research up to that point, "judicial interaction with the agency falls along a continuum, ranging from cases with little or no judicial involvement that triggered changes in the EPA, to cases involving active and aggressive judges that also triggered changes in the EPA (O'Leary 1995, 152). Her research contributes to theory building in the broad area of public administration and the law.

Other examples of interpretive analysis can be seen in the context of feminist theory, which tends to rely predominantly on content analysis, narratives, hermeneutics, and grounded theory.[11] Grounded theory is a qualitative research methodology whereby theory is generated from data rather than vice versa.[12] One of the most prominent public administration researchers who has written in all these traditions is Camilla Stivers, whose work has greatly advanced the field's body of knowledge from a feminist perspective (also see Ferguson 1984). Stivers's feminist discourse, which bridges interpretivism, empiricism, and postmodernism, has appeared frequently in the public administration literature and most notably in two of her books: *Gender Images in Public Administration* (Stivers 1992, 2002) and *Bureau Men, Settlement Women: Constructing Public Administration in the Progressive Era* (Stivers 2000). In both books, she relies on a mixture of hermeneutics, grounded theory, and content and critical analyses (also see Stivers 2005).

In *Gender Images in Public Administration*, Stivers illustrates that the field of public administration evolved in a way where male culture has dominated and has been valued over women's to the detriment of the field. The culture of the administrative state associates images of management, leadership, and public virtue with masculinity. Thus, everything is measured against the standards defined and created by men. Stivers (2002, 3) states that "images of professional expertise, management, leadership, and public virtue . . . not only have features commonly and unthinkingly associated with masculinity but they also help to keep in place or bestow political and economic privilege on the bearers of masculine qualities at the expense of those who display culturally feminine ones."

In her follow-up book *Bureau Men, Settlement Women*, Stivers carefully examines the historical nature and contributions of work from a gender standpoint to illustrate how the field's evolution created, sanctioned, and legitimized gender biases. The domination of men in the independent research bureau, the New York Bureau of Municipal Research, and its preoccupation with the science of administration overshadowed the contributions of women, who were largely consigned to settlement houses, which sought to help the urban poor. Science and rationality, reflected in the role of men in the rise of the administrative state, vanquished the social work role of women, which underscored caring and nurturing. Stivers asked, "What would public administration and public service have looked like had masculinity not prevailed?" The research of other scholars has also contributed greatly to feminist theory in public administration, including that of Guy (1993), Hutchinson (2005), Hutchinson and Mann (2004, 2006), Burnier (2006), Duerst-Lahti and Kelly (1995), Shields (2005, 2006), Horiuchi (2005), Rusaw (2005), and McGinn and Patterson (2005).

A final example of qualitative methods in the tradition of interpretivism can be seen in ethnography.[13] Developed by anthropologists, ethnography is common in all social sciences. In ethnographic studies, the researcher, when gathering data, is a participant in the study or situation. Its primary premise is to observe how people behave in their own environments. In the context of public administration, McNabb (2002, 323) observes that typically, "ethnographic studies are carried out in the inner cities of modern societies, in suburban and rural settings in cross-cultural communities, and in large and small organizations; the purpose is to investigate the many ways that the social forces of culture an subculture impact people." A number of scholars have conducted ethnographic studies (see Selden, Sowa, and Sandfort 2006; Sandfort 2000, 2003; Maynard-Moody, Stull, and Mitchell 1986; Rhodes 2005; and Brower, Abolafia, and Carr 2000).

Jodi Sandfort's research relies heavily on ethnographic methods, and it has contributed greatly to theory building in public administration.[14] In her intensive study of welfare culture, she finds a disconnect between management frameworks and the day-to-day operations of frontline workers in welfare offices operated by government as well as private contractors (also see Riccucci 2005). Through the application of social theory she finds that "there is an ongoing social process not capitalized upon by existing management approaches" (Sandfort 2000, 729). She concludes with a set of propositions that could potentially improve managerial actions on the front lines of service delivery.

Carolyn Ban's 1995 *How Do Public Managers Manage? Bureaucratic Constraints, Organizational Culture, and the Potential for Reform* provides an ethnographic study of the effect of organizational culture on managers' behavior in four U.S. federal agencies. It provides a rare look at the internal workings of federal agencies in terms of problem solving and the managing of human resources in the context of bureaucratic constraint. Ban's extensive research contributes significantly to the body of literature on the positive impact of effective management on program success.

Although not squarely in the area of public administration, Mitchel Abolafia's 1996 book *Making Markets: Opportunism and Restraint on Wall Street* represents an ethnographic study of Wall Street culture. He shows markets to be socially constructed institutions that operate not as objective leviathans or juggernauts but rather subjectively, based on the norms and customs of traders who are often seeking to advance their own interests. His analysis is based on more than ten years of ethnographic research, during which he trained as a futures trader, conducting fieldwork on trading floors, in order to gain firsthand knowledge of the behavior of financial markets from the traders themselves.[15]

In sum, these examples are illustrative of some of the qualitative research methods in the interpretivist tradition. Interpretive studies offer rich, contextual, and conceptual depth and represent one viable approach to theory building in public administration. Again, however, it must be stressed that there are overlapping qualities in these traditions. For example, not only interpretivists but also postmodernists and empiricists rely upon ethnographic research methods.

RATIONALISM

As discussed in chapter 4, rationalism is the philosophic view of acquiring knowledge through reason; that is, reason, not experience or sense perceptions, is the chief source of knowing or arriving at the truth. Rationalists believe in the logical power of the mind; a phenomenon can be so clear logically and mathematically that we know it to be true.[16] Spicer (1995, 14) states that the "rationalist worldview sees men and women, potentially at least, as possessing substantial powers of reason and able to use that reason intentionally to improve outcomes of humanity."

Early philosophers such as Descartes maintained that the human mind was capable of knowing the existence of God, but nothing else. He believed that human knowledge derived from the intellect operating independently of the senses. Spinoza held that only reason could reveal truth and that only God was the guarantee of knowledge. He utilized geometrical methods to arrive at the truth; for him, knowledge could only emanate from self-evident truths revealed by mathematics.

Rationalism in public administration was evident in early scholarship in the field. As Spicer (1995, 26–27) notes:

> Early public administration writers had a deep faith in the power of reason and its role in human progress. They were profoundly influenced by doctrines . . . emphasiz[ing] the powers of reason to order human affairs. Woodrow Wilson captured [the] philosophical outlook best when he argued that "man by using his intellect can remake society, that he can become the creator of a world organized for man's advantage" (Waldo 1984, 18). Public administration was seen by early writers as an instrument of collective intellect or of collective reason. Herman Finer (1925, 278) made explicit the role of the state in the application of reason when he observed that the civil service "acts on the theory that the good of the individual and of society may be discovered by the processes of social reason and action and be implemented through statutes."

Critical thinking and reasoning tend to be the methodological approaches for rationalists writing in public administration, as represented in conceptual analysis and normative discourse. Scholars writing on the new public administration serve as an example. Spearheaded by Dwight Waldo, public administration scholars convened at the Minnowbrook Conference Center in upstate New York to question public administration's significance or relevance in the context of the 1960s zeitgeist. Young scholars in the field argued for the significance for public administration of such values as social equity, representativeness, and social responsibility. They also called for a value-driven public administration, arguing that public administrators *ought to* react and respond to social change and should act as advocates and change agents for their clients rather than in the politically neutral fashion called for by the classical theorists. Researchers, they also maintained, ought to have a social agenda and not strive for neutrality. Arguing that social equity, for example, is a significant value of public administration and should be pursued reflects the value orientation of the new public administrationists. The various contributions in Marini's *Toward a New Public Administration*, which captured the themes and essence of the conference, are illustrative. For example, Frederickson (1971) advanced the seminal theoretical justifications for social equity as a critical value in public administration (also see Frederickson 1974, 1980, 1990). He reasoned that "the procedures of representative democracy presently operate in a way that either fails or only very gradually attempts to reverse systematic discrimination against disadvantaged minorities. Social equity, then, includes activities designed to enhance the political power and economic well being of these minorities" (Frederickson 1971, 311).

Samuel Krislov's 1974 classic volume *Representative Bureaucracy* is another example here.[17] Krislov addresses the importance of representative bureaucracy from a normative perspective, reasoning that it improves the process of governing because policies will be more reflective of a wide diversity of views. This in turn promotes democratic legitimacy. Krislov (1974, 130) argues that the "homogenized bureaucracies run the risk of getting better and better at performing tasks which other people regard as of increasingly less importance. When new winds sweep through such structures, they not only infuse fresh thoughts. By their momentum they also have the potential of spreading the effectiveness and purpose of the structure, so that its external reach is extended."

Krislov also poses an important question that helped shape research agendas in the area of representative bureaucracy: Will representative bureaucracies lead to representative public policies? That is, are passive and active representativeness linked? Krislov (1974, 40) reasons that representative bureaucracies will have such an effect, arguing that diversity in the workforce "dictates and reflects policy." He leaves this question open for future research, especially of an explanatory or logical positivist nature, examples of which are presented in chapter 6.

A more recent example of normative discourse in the field can be seen in Bertelli and Lynn's (2006) *Madison's Managers: Public Administration and the Constitution*. They propose a constitutional theory of public administration. Building on the work of Rosenbloom, Rohr, and others, Bertelli and Lynn (2006, x) suggest that managerial responsibility ought to depend, "in a constitutional sense, on official respect for the separation of powers and commitment to specific public services values: judgment, balance, rationality, and accountability." In their normative analysis, they go on to say that "focusing on these axiomatic values rehabilitates the theoretical and practical importance of two long-neglected aspects of public administration: the personnel function . . . and administrative law." The Madisonian theme that runs throughout their discourse is that public management should be "an entity . . . controlled in the bargaining among the separate powers and organized interests within the polity" (Bertelli and Lynn 2006, x).

Bertelli and Lynn analyze the early writings in the field and conclude that these early treatises were significant to theory building in public administration. Almost in an interpretivist tradition, they argue that many of the early critiques of public administrative theory were off the mark because they failed to interpret the texts within their rightful historical and institutional contexts, "as if their originators' reasons for responding as they did to the administrative problems of their day are of no intrinsic intellectual or practical interest" (Bertelli and Lynn 2006, 15). Interpreting texts within a historical context is critical for their main purpose, which is "theoretical, even philosophical, not historical. But theorizing in public administration needs historical perspective: ideas and arguments in their cultural, intellectual and institutional contexts" (Bertelli and Lynn 2006, 16).

Another example of rationalism through critical thinking and reasoning is Rosenbloom's (1983b) *Public Administration Review* article, "Public Administrative Theory and the Separation of Powers." In this insightful piece, Rosenbloom, building on the work of Kaufman (1956), argues that public administrative theory has three competing approaches: managerial, political, and legal. Or public administration can be defined as management, politics, and law. Each approach has a unique origin, set of values, and organizing structures. The managerial approach, for example, grew out of the civil service reform movement of the late nineteenth century and values efficiency, effectiveness, and economy. In contrast, the political approach, growing out of challenges to the politics/administration dichotomy, places emphasis on such values as responsiveness, accountability, and representativeness, whereas the legal approach, emanating from efforts to promote the importance of law to public administration, embodies due process and equal treatment. Although conflicting, Rosenbloom reasons that the approaches are analogous to the U.S. Constitution's separation of powers in that each is inextricably essential to the enterprise of public administration—as the separation of powers are to the governing of the nation—and each serves as a check on the other approaches, as do the three branches of government. This critical analysis by Rosenbloom greatly advanced our knowledge and understanding of the origins and nature of the field of public administration.

The field of system dynamics and the somewhat moribund design sciences represent other areas steeped in rationalism (see Shangraw and Crow 1989).[18] System dynamics, which relies on mathematical reasoning, refers to computer-based modeling methods to help achieve policy consensus in complex dynamic environments. In particular, it relies on information-feedback structures, or loops, to maximize decision-making processes. The subject area is an outlier in the field of public administration and is somewhat generic and boutique-ish.[19] Moreover, one rarely finds articles on system dynamics in public administrative journals. But there are a handful of researchers in schools or departments of public administration, affairs, or policy across the country that work in the area.

For example, George Richardson, a mathematician by training, writes extensively in the area of system dynamics, in particular, exploring the theoretical justifications for systems thinking. In his book *Feedback Thought in Social Science and Systems Theory*, Richardson (1991) propounds that there are two main threads in feedback thinking: cybernetics, the theoretical study of control and communication systems through mathematical analysis of the flow of information; and servomechanisms, an automatic device for sensing errors and providing feedback to resolve or correct the performance of a system or mechanism. The work of Richardson as well as others in system dynamics clearly promotes a generic, apolitical, instrumental, and rationalist view of systems thinking.

Adams and Balfour's (2004) book *Unmasking Administrative Evil*—now in its third edition (2009)—represents a conceptual and metaethical analysis in the rationalist tradition. "Metaethics" refers to efforts to comprehend and assess the epistemological, semantic, metaphysical, and psychological presuppositions of moral thought and practice. In the context here, Adams and Balfour examine the moral responsibility—or the underlying morality—of administrators, who carry out administrative orders, no matter how personably objectionable, that under any conceivable or imaginable moral circumstance represent evil. Their book advanced public administrative theory in new, uncharted ways. In fact, Charles Perrow, in his foreword to the revised edition of the book, states that it "makes one realize how much organizational theory (and worse yet, public administration theory) has largely ignored, or sanitized, the notion of evil" (Adams and Balfour 2004, ix).

Adams and Balfour probe the question, What is it about modern organizations that allow evil to be administered in a technically rational, efficient manner? They answer this question partly in the context of the Shoah, more commonly called the Holocaust, Nazi Germany's rational, bureaucratic mass extermination or genocide of the Jews. The Holocaust is a clear example of administrative evil unmasked. Adams and Balfour's work shows that even in contemporary administrative settings, evil is present and can be enacted. The task for public administration is to unmask administrative evil in particular by breaking down traditional organizational systems and structures that thrive on technical rationality. Their research advances the body of knowledge on ethics and morality in public administration.

One final example of rationalism from a critical analysis perspective can be seen in Terry Moe's work on the applicability of agency theory to government. Agency theory, or principal–agent theory, embodies power relationships between legislative bodies and bureaucratic agencies. In essence, it takes bureaucratic politics theory away from political science in the direction of economics or more precisely microeconomics. In his classic article "The New Economics of Organization," Moe (1984, 739) states that this "approach has emerged from recent attempts to move beyond the neoclassical theory of the firm, which assumes away all organizational considerations, to a theory of economic organizations that can explain why firms, corporations, and other enterprises behave as they do." He goes on to say that "the more general principal–agent models of hierarchical control have shown that, under a range of conditions, the principal's optimal incentive structure for the agent is one in which the latter receives some share of the residual payment for his efforts, thus giving him a direct stake in the outcome. . . . For public bureaucracy, however, there is no residual in the ordinary sense of the term. The typical bureau receives a budget from governmental superiors and spends all of it supplying services to a nonpaying clientele" (Moe 1984, 763). He says further that "slack" serves as one critical proxy; slack is the difference between the true cost of service provision and what the agency actually spends. It represents resources that agency leaders can have internal control over, thus providing an incentive for controlling bureaucratic behavior.

And how does the principal–agent model adjust itself in terms of the relationship between elected representatives—the "politicians"—and the bureaucrats? Moe argues that the "model offers a simple reinterpretation of the traditional problem of administration accountability." Moe, laying the groundwork for further research, suggests quid pro quo mechanisms between the elected officials and the career bureaucrats, such as appropriation and apportionment controls over the budget. His work here as well as elsewhere represents a major contribution to research and the literature in the area principal–agent theory.

There are many other examples of research in the tradition of rationalism with a reliance on critical analysis or normative discourse. Spicer (1995), for example, points to the works of DiIulio (1989) writing on public management and administrative arrangements, Wamsley (1990) on agency theory, and Schick (1966) on rational systems of budgeting.

EMPIRICISM

Empiricism is a philosophy that supports the existence of reality and knowledge through experiences, in particular sensory perceptions. English philosophers such as John Locke reacted critically to the rationalism espoused by Descartes and his contemporaries. To Locke the mind was tabula rasa, a blank slate to be filled by experiences of the senses as opposed to abstract reasoning and speculation. Locke, along with the Irish bishop George Berkeley and the Scottish philosopher David Hume, shared the view that there could be no innate ideas, present from birth, apart from experience; the mind is not capable of possessing ideas without being *aware* of those ideas.[20]

Hawkesworth (2006, 29) offers this observation about empiricism: "The senses function as faithful recording devices, placing before the 'mind's eye' exact replicas of that which exists in the external world, without cultural or linguistic mediation. Precisely because observation is understood as exact replication, strategies for the acquisition of knowledge are said to be 'neutral' and 'value free.' In this view, scientific investigations can grasp objective reality, because the subjectivity of individual observers can be controlled through rigid adherence to neutral procedures."

One great myth associated with empiricism is that its methods are quantitative, when in fact empirical research is just as frequently conducted with qualitative methods. In addition, empiricism is sometimes treated analogously to positivism (see, e.g., Hawkesworth 2006); for the purposes of this book, they are treated separately (see table 4.1 for further comparisons).[21] This chapter addresses empiricism through qualitative methods, and chapter 6 presents empirical research in the context of quantitative methods. Chapter 7 presents empirical research in the context of mixed methods.

Qualitative methods for empirical research include, for example, case studies, field studies, narratives, storytelling, and the much-maligned best practices approach.[22] Case studies, a popular approach of empiricists, can be single or multiple.[23] Van Evera (1997) points to five uses for case studies in public administration: to create theories; to test previously established theories; to identify antecedent conditions; to test the importance of these antecedent conditions, and to explain cases of intrinsic importance. Classic case studies that have had a tremendous impact on the study of public administration include Herbert Kaufman's (1960) *The Forest Ranger: A Study in Administrative Behavior* and Michael Lipsky's (1980) *Street-Level Bureaucracy: Dilemmas of the Individual in Public Services.*

Kaufman's case study examines the administrative behaviors of lower-level bureaucrats, forest rangers, in the U.S. Forest Service. His in-depth research looks at five ranger districts to determine how the behaviors and actions of forest rangers compare with or conform to the policy directives of agency leaders. In his 2007 book review of *The Forest Ranger,* Luton (2007b, 165) states that Kaufman's case study "stands as an example of how to do research that has a lasting impact. First published in 1960, it remains relevant almost 50 years later." Luton goes on to say that it "remains one of the most frequently cited case studies in public administration—a field in which the case study is one of the most often used research approaches (Jensen and Rodgers 2001) . . . [and] is a model of how to conduct a public administration case study." Kaufman's research has had an enormous impact on public administration literature in several areas, including decision making, administrative behavior, and public management.

Lipsky's seminal research on street-level bureaucrats is equally timeless. He coined the term "street-level bureaucrat" to refer to those government employees working on the front lines of service delivery (e.g., police officers and social workers). He showed how street-level bureaucrats are faced with dilemmas in their jobs because of the vast amount of discretion they wield in the execution of their work, which ultimately has implications for government accountability. He found that street-level bureaucrats possess a major source of power and are integral in the implementation of public policy. It is an understatement to say that his work has been critical to theory building in public administration.

There are a number of qualitatively empirical studies on street-level bureaucrats relying on such methods as case studies and narratives (e.g.,

Prottas 1979; Vinzant and Crothers 1998; Riccucci 2007a). One study written in the tradition of storytelling can be seen in the cogent work of Maynard-Moody and Musheno (2003), *Cops, Teachers, Counselors: Stories from the Front Lines of Public Service*. As the title of their book suggests, they gathered detailed stories and interviews over a period of three years from three cohorts of street-level bureaucrats: police officers, teachers, and vocational rehabilitation counselors. A total of forty-eight street-level workers at five sites in two states (one in the Southwest, one in the Midwest) were included in their study. Storytelling allows the researchers to delve deeply into the world of a study's subject, and it provides for an in-depth explanation of the logic of behavioral patterns.[24]

Maynard-Moody and Musheno (2003, 26) first point out that "storytelling, like the diorama, is an act of 'world-building' and 'world-populating.' Hearing a story, we enter, if only for a moment, this created world and interact with its characters. Street-level workers' stories re-created their world as they see it and as they want to present it to outsiders."

Narratives and storytelling are often treated synonymously (e.g., Ospina and Dodge 2005). However, Maynard-Moody and Musheno (2003, 26–27) draw a distinction between the two methods. They state that the

> narrative is the broader category: all stories are narratives, but all narratives are not stories. The various textual forms of qualitative social science, such as ethnographies, folk tales, case studies, observations, and other similar accounts, are forms of narratives. . . . Our working definition of *story* is close to the traditional everyday use of the word. . . . We strive to collect stories that have plot lines, however simple or tenuous, and that exist in time. . . . They have a beginning, . . . a middle, . . . and an end that brings the events to their logical or surprise conclusions. . . . Good research stories provide details about events and setting. They also tell us about the characters and their interactions, relationships and feelings. . . . The details that make the characters vivid are the textual embodiments of the storytellers' judgments about the characters and events.

The stories collected and analyzed by Maynard and Musheno tell us that the behaviors of street-level bureaucrats are influenced not by bureaucratic rules and regulations but rather by their own moral judgments, which are based on their personal knowledge of and constant interactions with clients. Maynard-Moody and Musheno (2003, 93–94) find that "moral judgments about citizen-clients infuse all aspects of street-level decision making. To street-level workers, fairness has little to do with the bureaucratic norm of treating everyone the same or even fairly implementing laws and regulations. To our storytellers, fairness and justice mean responding to citizen-clients based on their perceived worth." This is a critical finding, and runs counter to much of the Weberian school of thought that so permeates public administration. Overall, their research greatly advances public administrative theory in the area of street-level bureaucracy.

Other examples of qualitative empiricism with a reliance on case studies can be seen in the work of Milward and Provan (1993, 2000) on the "hollow state" (also see Brudney 1990).[25] The hollow state is a metaphor for the use of third parties, particularly nonprofits, to deliver government services and act on behalf of the state (Milward and Provan 2000). In one of their earliest studies, Milward and Provan (1993) examine a community's mental health network in Tucson and Pima County, Arizona, to determine the degree to which it has been hollowed out. They note that the concept of the hollow state grew out of the "hollow corporation," whose story was covered in a 1986 special report by *Business Week* (1986). Through their extensive analysis of the community mental health system, they found evidence supporting the hollowing out of the state as major functions and tasks are turned over to contractors. This, they conclude, has implications for how public services are delivered as well as for citizens' overall perceptions of government.

Field studies represent another example of methods for qualitatively based empirical studies. A field study is a descriptive research approach where the researcher spends time in the field (e.g., in an organization or group of organizations) collecting and analyzing observations, surveys, interviews, and agency documents.[26] It allows for in-depth research so that contextual factors not readily apparent or visible can be accounted for. One example can be seen in Connell's (2006) field study of gender divisions at worksites in New South Wales, Australia.[27] Connell conducted an in-depth field study of ten worksites in this oldest, most populous state in Australia. At the time of her study, the Australian Labor Party, a social-democratic party similar to the British Labour Party, controlled New South Wales. She observes that although gender equity has been a critical component of the public-sector reform movement in Australia, women have made little progress in the country's Parliament or other public bodies such as the Senior Executive Service. This initial observation motivated her to study the representation of women in the New South Wales government. She studied two worksites for each of the five agencies (which were not named) targeted for her research. Her fieldwork extended over a period of eighteen months and involved interviews and participant observations. She interviewed a total of fifty-eight women and forty-nine men from all levels and all occupational groups at each worksite.

Connell begins by setting up a framework that goes beyond traditional studies of gender equity, which in large part seek to determine the extent to which women occupy upper levels of organizational hierarchies. She instead examines the pattern of gender relations within organizations, a phenomenon she dubs its "gender regime." She points out that a gender regime has four major dimensions: (1) gender divisions of labor, or the gendering of occupations and the division between paid and domestic labor; (2) gender relations of power, or how control and authority are exercised along gender lines; (3) emotion and human relations, or how feelings and emotions are organized along gender lines; and (4) gender culture and symbolism, reflecting beliefs and attitudes about gender and gender roles.

Connell's fieldwork approach allowed for a richer, multidimensional picture of gender within organizations. Her findings show that similar to patterns in the United States, gender divisions exist along occupational lines within the New South Wales government. Her research also found that women managers often lack legitimate authority, in the sense that men will not follow their directives; the transition of women into higher-level posts, she reports, resulted in ill-feelings and resentment by men and "degendering," or a lack of recognition or acceptance of differences in gender cultures.

Another empirically based, qualitative research approach is best practices, which has been maligned in some corners of public administration and management as the nadir of research traditions. As the name implies, best practices research seeks out examples of efficacy and success in government, such as in leadership, management capacity, innovation, and administrative reform. Its aim is to exemplify. Applied fields such as public administration have made extensive use of best practices research in an effort to bridge the gap between theory and practice for practitioners.[28] Bardach (1994, 260), pointing to the "legitimate reason" for this type of research, states: "The goal of 'best practice' research . . . is widening the range of solutions to problems."

In support of best practices research, Lynn (1994, 245) argues that "public management scholarship in the public policy community should continue to claim as its domain the executive function in government; as its approach, the observation and documentation of best practice by managerial actors; and as its focus, the identification and achievement of the aims of public policy." Quoting Vickers (1983, 67), Lynn (1994, 246) goes on to justify best practices research by stating that "identifying 'best' practices involves discrimination or, as Sir Geoffrey Vickers says, appreciative judgments, by which he means 'a set of readiness to distinguish some aspects of the situation rather than others and to classify and value these in this way rather than that.'"

Best practices research relies primarily on case studies, narratives, and extensive, in-depth field research.[29] Cooper and Wright's (1992) *Exemplary Public Administrators: Character and Leadership in Government* is a good example. Their book includes profiles on several important figures in public administration, including Paul Appleby, Robert Moses, Elsa Porter, and Elmer Staats. Cooper and Wright (1992, xi–xii) begin by noting that their "book offers character studies of eleven public administrators whom the authors propose as exemplary and as living evidence that high ethical standards in public life can be achieved. The emphasis is on 'telling the stories' of each." The narratives are intended to provide rich, in-depth examples of exactly how the eleven public administrators promote ethical behaviors in their work lives. Through each case study, "the viability of an ethic of public administration grounded in the concept of virtue" is examined and identified.

Cooper and Wright (1992, xii–xiii) also point to another critical purpose of best practices research: It serves as an educational tool. They note that profiles of exemplary administrators provide "instructive and inspirational role models both for preservice students considering careers in public service and for working administrators in a field that often feels maligned and demeaned by the public and the media. Similarly, this project could be an effective means for projecting a more positive image of public service to the citizenry." In addition, countering bureaucrat bashing serves as a strong justification for exemplary profiles, particularly for those committed to the practice and study of public administration.

Another example of best practices research can be seen in Rainey and Thompson's (2006) profile of Charles Rossotti, who served as commissioner of the Internal Revenue Service.[30] Their careful, insightful examination of Rossotti's tenure in that role illustrated how his leadership skills improved the agency's image and ultimately services to American taxpayers. The creation of a leadership team, leading and overseeing improvements in information technology capabilities, and the skillful implementation of legislatively imposed reforms were some of the strategies on which Rossotti relied in overhauling the Internal Revenue Service and bringing positive, sustainable change to the manner in which the agency provides services.

Best practices research can also focus on programs, as seen in Behn's (1991) examination of Massachusetts' welfare, training, and employment program, ET Choices (ET refers to employment and training), during the Michael Dukakis gubernatorial administration; the program sought to move welfare recipients off welfare and into jobs. Of course, it is the *people* behind the programs who drive success, and Behn focuses on them as well. One of his findings is that private-sector management techniques do not readily apply to the public sector. Another important contribution of his case study is the advancement of his management concept "groping along." Behn (1991, 133–34) states that " 'groping along' accurately describes the process by which any organization creates sentences, phrases, and words it uses to describe its purposes. Conversely, this managerial search for words provides a useful metaphor for describing the process of management: 'Management by Groping Along,' or MBGA." He goes on to say that "despite years of experience and study, even the best manager must grope along. . . . Rather than develop a detailed study to be followed unswervingly, a good manager establishes a specific direction—a very clear objective—and then gropes his way toward it. He knows where he is trying to go but is not sure how to get there. So he tries a lot of different things. Some work. Some do not. . . . Finally what works best begins to take hold. This is management by groping along."

Behn also argues that efficacy in achieving public goals requires managers to pursue a combination of policy, administrative, and leadership metastrategies. He observes, however, that while "anyone who seeks to accomplish public purposes will have to employ some combination of all three approaches . . . those in government tend to rely most heavily on just one of these three metastrategies while ignoring the other two" (Behn 1991, 198). He ultimately concludes in his very comprehensive, systematic analysis that "leadership counts" in the successful management of public programs and policies.

Harvard University's John F. Kennedy School of Government promotes best practices research with its Innovations in American Government Awards Program, which "identifies and promotes best practices and exemplary projects that can be adopted in other settings, providing public officials and senior executives with innovative leadership models" (Ash Center for Democratic Governance and Innovation 2009). More than 300 government programs have been profiled as best practices since the award's inception in 1986.

POSTPOSITIVISM

The prefix "post" in "postpositivism" is somewhat misleading, in that postpositivism is not the next iteration, nor a mere alteration, of positivism. Indeed, it rejects the tenets of positivism. Unlike positivists, postpositivists maintain that all observation is imperfect or fallible and subject to inaccuracies. Science and research can strive to reach reality, but that goal can never be realized. Critical realism is the most notable manifestation of postpositivism. And as the name implies, the critical realist is critical of our capacity or even ability to know reality with certainty.

As noted in chapter 4, Karl Popper, a proponent of postpositivism, maintained that human knowledge could only be gained through empirical falsification. Propositions could be disproved or falsified but never proven correct, because of the possibility of always disproving them. Fischer (1998, 129) points out that "as a discursive orientation grounded in practical reason, the postpositivist approach situates empirical inquiry in a broader interpretive framework. More than just an epistemological alternative, the approach is offered as a better description of what social scientists actually do in practice."

Postpositivism has traditionally been based in qualitative traditions, and this has especially been the case for public administration. But many have argued that postpositivism is based not only in qualitative but also in quantitative and mixed methods.[31] Creswell (2009, 6–7; emphasis added), for example, has argued that "postpositivist assumptions have represented the traditional form of research, and these assumptions hold true more for quantitative research than qualitative research. . . . Postpositivists hold a deterministic philosophy in which causes *probably* determine effects of outcomes." It thus begins with the premise that knowledge is imperfect and fallible, that absolute truth is beyond the researcher's grasp. As Gabrielian, Yang, and Spice (2008, 144) point out, postpositivism has "a greater tolerance for error—the findings would be probable, rather than established and verified laws; they would be considered true until falsified."

As noted in chapter 4 (specifically, table 4.1), examples of postpositive research can be seen in narratives, storytelling, ethnography, participatory policy analysis, and Q methodology.[32] Only examples of participatory policy analysis and Q methodology will be offered in this section, for the others are addressed elsewhere in this chapter.[33] (Chapter 7 addresses the use of mixed methods within a postpositivist framework.) The key, whether postpositivist ethnography, narrative, or another tradition, is that the locus of the research is recognized as a social and political laboratory, of which the researcher is an integral part. The researcher is considered an informed subject, just like the actual research subjects, and thus is implicated in the generation of data.

Participatory policy analysis, as Fischer (2003, 15) points out, involves "deliberative interactions between citizens, analysts, and decision makers." He goes on to say that participatory inquiry is of particular interest to postpositivists or postempiricists, because "in its various forms [it] has the possibility of bringing to the fore both new knowledge—in particular local knowledge—and normative interpretations that are unavailable to more abstract empirical methods typically removed from the subjects of inquiry. . . . Indeed, its ability to deliver firsthand knowledge of the circumstances of a local context addresses a major limitation of conventional methods, a central concern of postempirical analysis" (Fischer 2003, 206).[34]

Haight and Ginger's (2000) case study of the Vermont Forest Resources Advisory Council (FRAC) in the mid-1990s serves as an example of participatory policy inquiry. FRAC is a citizen advisory body created in 1977 to advise the legislature and governor of Vermont on forest issues. At the time, it was comprised of about fifteen members, and involved about forty stakeholders, representing public and private interests in forestry, industry, wildlife, environmental sciences, conservation, and the general citizenry. It has been charged with a number of contentious issues in the state, including clear-cutting and aerial herbicide spraying in forests.[35] Public sentiment runs very high on the issues, and the outcomes of FRAC's work potentially affect social, economic, and even biological conditions in Vermont.

Haight and Ginger's examination focused on the degree to which FRAC promoted trust and understanding in the policy process. Through observation, extensive interviews, and an examination of citizen comments, meeting minutes, and agency documents, they found that certain processes employed by FRAC reduced tensions and promoted trust among stakeholders. One process was the creation of working groups reflecting a diverse array of perspectives and interests. FRAC also promoted an inclusive and open style of communication and management. It held public hearings and open meetings with interested parties and encouraged a spirit of collaboration. Stakeholders were also able to explore issues on field trips to logging operations and lumber mills.

FRAC also promoted trust and understanding through collaboration by creating a roundtable format for decision making. Haight and Ginger also found that FRAC became more cognizant of social values such as health, private property, and aesthetics as they related to forestry issues. As an advisory body, FRAC had customarily depended on scientific information as a basis for its recommendations. The level of openness and multilateral communications ultimately led to a more democratic approach to policy discussions and ultimately to FRAC's recommendations with respect to pivotal forestry matters in Vermont.

Another example of participatory policy inquiry can be seen in Durning's 1993 study of Georgia's Division of Rehabilitation Service (DRS), which provides financial and other assistance to disabled persons seeking jobs. His case study involved an examination of DRS employees who were members of a team analyzing a policy, known as "order of selection" (OS), which sets priorities for potential recipients of services from the agency. The appointment of a team as opposed to a single policy analyst was a standard operating procedure for DRS. The agency also prided itself on the practice of obtaining advice from the clients it served. The intake process for DRS caseworkers involved a determination of whether applicants qualified for the OS disability category for which funds were available. If qualified, the caseworker then works with the client to develop a plan to prepare for employment. The DRS pays for all financial expenses associated with this task. The caseworkers had a degree of discretion in making their decisions here; although the authorizing law stipulates that the highest priority be given to "severely handicapped" persons, it did not define what constitutes "severely." The OS policy was designed to provide some guidance to caseworkers in prioritizing applicants for aid. (It may have also been intended to circumscribe the discretionary powers of street-level workers.) It was an unpopular policy, principally because caseworkers felt that it did not do an adequate job of assisting them in making their determinations for funding.

The team assembled to analyze the efficacy of the OS policy comprised caseworkers, supervisors, two assistant directors, and other staff members of the DRS. Durning provides a detailed examination of the various steps taken by the project team, including comparing the OS policy with those policies employed in other states, brainstorming ways to improve the policy, working with caseworkers to develop alternative strategies, and surveying directors for their input. The team ultimately developed three alternatives to the OS policy with various scenarios for ramifications for implementation.

Durning concludes from his observations and analysis that participatory policy inquiry informs practice and research on such matters as small group behavior, knowledge utilization and analytic credibility (i.e., the acceptance of participatory inquiry as compared with traditional, positivist types of policy analysis such as cost/benefit), participative program evaluation, and collaborative policymaking. He concludes with the following strengths of participatory policy analysis: (1) a more thorough understanding of the context of policy and analysis by the team; (2) the values of diversity in opinions, data, and information from the "experts"; (3) a multitude of perspectives to increase the ability to predict potential consequences of proposed policy alternatives; and (4) increased credibility within the DRS. Durning concludes that participatory inquiry is an important method for analyzing policy matters within organizations.

Q methodology, sometimes referred to as q sorts, is another example of research in the tradition of postpositivism. It was developed by Stephenson (1935a, 1935b, 1953) to focus on persons, not tests. Q methodology is a tool that uncovers and systematically reveals subjective perspectives (e.g., persons' views, attitudes, and opinions), thus leading to improved policy-making, implementation, and evaluation (Steelman and Maguire 1999). Durning (1999, 391) simply defines it as "a method for the study of subjectivity." The "Q" refers to an inversion of conventional factor analysis that challenges the assumptions of objectivism associated with R-methods. It has been used in a number of social science disciplines or fields, including sociology, psychology, social psychology, political science, political psychology, and public administration (Selden, Brewer, and Brudney 1999; Durning and Osuna 1994; Cunningham and Olshfski 1986; Brown 1980).

Van Exel and de Graaf (2005, 4) observe that "in a Q methodological study people are presented with a sample of statements about some topic, called the Q-set. Respondents, called the P-set, are asked to rank-order the statements from their individual point of view, according to some preference, judgment or feeling about them, mostly using a quasi-normal distribution. By Q sorting, people give their subjective meaning to the statements, and by doing so reveal their subjective viewpoint . . . or personal profile."

Durning and Osuna (1994) use Q methodology in their study of policy analysts and researchers in three states—California, Georgia, and Arkansas—across the country, seeking to identify how they define their roles in organizations as well as society, and how, taking into account their professional responsibilities and their interactions with clients, they define the "public good."[36] They explain their research process as follows: "During the field administration, or Q-sort, participants demonstrate how they think and feel about a group of stimuli statements. The participant is presented with a Q-sample consisting of printed statements. How participants [the P-set] sort these statements along a continuum of valences ranging from extreme disagreement to extreme agreement communicates their 'operant subjectivity' at the time of administration" (Durning and Osuna 1994, 633–34).

Durning and Osuna (1994, 639) collected 118 statements from a variety of sources. Examples of statements include:

♦ Analysts should strive to be objective and value neutral.
♦ An analyst contributes to the good society, at least in the long run, by consistently providing unbiased advice, even when it does not lead to the selection of personally favored policies.
♦ Politics is somebody else's business. My main business is research, which is linked to policymaking.

Durning and Osuna asked the respondents, or the P-set, to rank order the statements from their personal perspective. They then formulated a two-dimensional factorial design to classify the representative sample of statements. The dimensions are "types of analysts or researchers" (objective technician; client advocate, or issue advocate) and "dimensions of roles and value orientations" (e.g., main responsibilities; to whom are you responsible; definitions of success, failure, and quality).

Their factor analysis revealed, for example, that policy analysts seek to balance the task of providing objective policy advice against the challenges of identifying the best solution to policy problems. They found that analysts must play the part of "political strategist," but they are reluctant to blindly follow political will. They also found that many researchers and policy analysts are unwilling to compromise analytic integrity in their work. Researchers tended to operate as objective technicians and, like policy analysts, are not overly "positivistic" in orientation. Durning and Osuna conclude by encouraging additional research using Q-methods.

In their study of national forest management, Steelman and Maguire (1999, 386) rely on Q methodology to determine whether public values are folded into decisions by policy analysts. They argue that Q methodology is a very useful approach for examining the degree to which public perspectives are actually incorporated into policy analysts' decision making. In short, their findings suggest that Q methodology has the "potential for lending sharper, more systematic insight into the values and preferences held by the public [which] could contribute to better problem identification and definition; estimation and specification of policy options; and selection, implementation and evaluation of policies."[37]

Callahan, Dubnick, and Olshfski (2006, 556) rely on Q methodology to study how public administrators processed war narratives offered by officials of the George W. Bush administration. War narratives, they state, capture "ideologies or schools of thought" about war and provide guidance and direction on appropriate behaviors and responses to war. They point out, for example, that the colonialists of New England relied on biblical narratives to "organize themselves in order to defend against the 'heathen tribes' that populated the continent." On the basis of their analysis of news coverage and political speeches on the "war on terror" that emanated from the September 11, 2001, terrorist attacks, they create four different war narratives:

- ◆ A garrison state narrative—preoccupation with national security, whereby society "organizes itself around the constant threat of war—it becomes a war machine" (Callahan, Dubnick, and Olshfski 2006, 558);
- ◆ A temporary state narrative—taking necessary but short-term measures during war;
- ◆ A glass firewall narrative—reflects civilian and military perspectives; during wartime, military expertise is relied upon, and civilians entrust the military with security and protection; and
- ◆ An enemy within narrative—national security threats operate within the nation's borders and must be expunged.

Callahan, Dubnick, and Olshfski developed a series of statements based on these narratives and asked respondents (ten middle- to upper-level public administrators from three separate public agencies[38]) to indicate how strongly they agree or disagree with each statement. As they point out, Q methodology "groups like-thinking individuals together, allowing researchers to determine how groups differ in their thinking and to examine the differences in characteristics and attributes among the groups" (Callahan, Dubnick, and Olshfski 2006, 559). Though they did not find distinct war narratives among the three groups, they found one group concerned primarily with civil liberties and another with vigilance or the need to avert future acts of terrorism and threats of war.

In sum, Q methodology is an approach to studying human subjectivity.[39] Though R-methods attempt to study the potential relationships between objective variables and patterns across those variables, Q-methods study patterns of subjective perspectives across persons or individuals (see Steelman and Maguire 1999).

As was noted above, triangulation, or mixed methods, is often relied upon in a postpositivist framework. Postpositivists believe it allows for multiple perspectives and thus enhances the ability to explain phenomena. Examples of the use of mixed methods are presented in chapter 7.

POSTMODERNISM

Postmodernism tends to be viewed as a radical concept because of its challenge to mainstream thought. Its emphasis on reasoning and freethinking has made it vulnerable to attack, particularly in academic circles. It has taken on a host of meanings, depending on the disciplinary context in which it appears, and indeed there is no consensus on an exact meaning. Nonetheless, from art to architecture, to film, music, literature, or sociology, postmodernists have made their unique imprint. In general, postmodernism posits that truth is in the eye of the beholder. In this sense, there are no universal truths and reality is a cultural and social construct. Miller and Fox (2006, ix), who have written extensively here, point out that postmodernism ruffles feathers in public administration because it "challenges mainstream presuppositions."[40] They go on to say that "postmodern thought calls into question institutions as we know them, and also challenges ontological presuppositions about society and the individual. Postmodernism treats skeptically the notion that autonomous liberal-humanist citizens, can, through public deliberation, come to agreement about what is real, much less what is desirable, and then effectuate their desires through current representative/democratic institutions. Business-as-usual public administration may not want to hear about the decohering of governing institutions" (Miller and Fox 2006, ix).

Yang, Zhang, and Holzer (2008, 26) point out that "postmodern approaches have expanded our understanding of . . . complex public administration phenomena." They go on to say that a postmodern framework can "help public administration researchers generate alternative understandings."

A host of books on public administration have been devoted to postmodernism, including, for example, Fox and Miller (1995), Miller (2002), Miller and Fox (2006), McSwite (1997, 2002), Spicer (2001), White (1999), and Yanow (2002). And, as discussed earlier in this chapter, Stivers's (2000, 2002) feminist critique of public administration challenges and deconstructs orthodox assumptions about the role of gender in the field of public administration. In addition, an entire journal, *Administrative Theory & Praxis*, extensively publishes postmodern critiques of public administration (see Box 2005).

Ralph Hummel (1996, 2006, 2007) has contributed immensely to the body of knowledge on postmodernism in public administration. In a 2006 essay Hummel asks whether a strong case can be made for postmodern analysis. He then sets forth "the question for policy, government, and administration of today: Is modern analysis, with its demand for categorical knowledge, capable of appropriate self-critique or is postmodern analysis, with its constant demand for re-examining the foundations, by definition better at it?" (Hummel 2006, 312). Through a careful and lively exploration of the philosophies of Kant, Foucault, Weber, Loewith, and Arendt, he points to the significant place of postmodern thought in public administration. But he also emphasizes the importance of tolerance in approaches and perspectives, a theme stressed throughout this book.

Evans and Wamsley (1999, 118) examine the field of public management from a postmodern perspective. They view public management as being "engaged in an ontological quest, though with varying degrees of consciousness." Moreover, they argue, public management has not been successful in achieving a consensus as to whether it is a field, discipline, interdisciplinary field, or applied field. They note that discovering the meaning of public management involves "existential questions," much like those "put so eloquently by Ross Perot's 1992 running mate, Admiral Stockdale: 'Who am I? And why am I here?'" (Evans and Wamsley 1999, 118).

Evans and Wamsley (1999, 117–18; emphasis in the original) rely on L. Frank Baum's classic 1900 tale *The Wizard of Oz* as a metaphor in their search for the meaning of public management, justifying their use of a metaphor in this fashion:

> Our understanding of self and the world, indeed human existence itself, is grounded in metaphors. Metaphors are the basis for our language and our ability to form abstractions. . . . Thus, the metaphor is a powerful tool for understanding and explaining complex ideas. . . . Although we acknowledge . . . potential dangers, we nonetheless believe that *The Wizard of Oz* has metaphorical power that can explain much that is troubling about public management today and can suggest some possible remedies. . . . We see *The Wizard of Oz* as an allegorical tale of a mythic journey in which the protagonists must overcome seemingly insurmountable obstacles to obtain what they *perceive* as missing in themselves. It is, in other words, the archetypal arduous journey of self-discovery that humankind has used to entertain and instruct going back as far as Homer's *Odyssey*.

Public management scholars, like Dorothy, are on a journey of self-discovery. They project "critical stereotypes onto one another, they make assumptions about what is missing in their and the others' research and practice, and both hope to find an all-powerful Wizard (a theory, a methodology, a concept) that can answer their ontological queries" (Evans and

Wamsley 1999, 119). They develop a variety of these analogies to assist them in their efforts to conceptualize public management. For example, the Emerald City, the fabled city of Oz, is public management's "state of false consciousness." False consciousness, derived from Marxist theory, refers to the institutional and material forces in a capitalist society, which lead to the failure of the lower social classes to comprehend their true role in society, and how they are exploited, subordinated and dominated by those processes and the higher classes.[41] Evans and Wamsley use the term in an ontological sense, whereby public management is unable to grasp its own self-identity and its level of importance in the world around us. They argue that public management as a lever of government should "go beyond serving the needs of a power elite, distributing largesse as the vector sum of interest group pressures or even as a corrective to market inadequacies" (Evans and Wamsley 1999, 122). Through additional analogies and applications of public administrative practices (e.g., reinventing government reforms to promote efficiency), they call for an "enhanced sense of community" as the key to "a vigorous renaissance in democratic theory" in our conceptualization of public management (Evans and Wamsley 1999, 137, 138).

Felts and Jos (2000) also rely on postmodern critique in their examination of the rise of the new public management (NPM). They argue that the philosophic underpinnings of the NPM rest in capitalism. They also note that the field of public administration has largely organized itself according to the precepts of capitalism. They state that "public bureaucracy owes at least part of its ascendancy to the demands of capitalist enterprise" (Felts and Jos 2000, 520). Quoting Weber, they go on to say, as "Weber (1968) noted a century ago, 'Today it is primarily the capitalist market economy which demands that the official business of public administration be discharged precisely, unambiguously, continuously, and with as much speed as possible'" (p. 520). They then ask, if capitalism, revered at the time, served as a basis for public administration, why are public administrationists so averse to the NPM today?

Their answer rests in the *globalization* of capitalism. Postindustrial, modern capitalism, they argue, must respond to the heightened demands of a global market, which calls for rapidity in adaptability, responsiveness, and flexibility. They state that unlike any other time in history, markets are much more consumer driven. They argue that the "market has become far too dynamic to allow the bureaucratic model of doing things the same way, year after year, or doing the same thing. Modern management texts emphasize the need for quick responsiveness in order to change as consumer preferences change or new technologies are introduced. Modern technologies communicate information at a speed beyond the imaginings of turn-of-the-century industrial capitalists" (Felts and Jos 2000, 523).

These modern demands of capitalism have, in part, discounted the virtues of bureaucracy in the American setting—such as a stable, tenured, highly skilled civil service—and replaced it with downsized, ad hoc, temporary work forces to staff short-term projects in response to rapidly changing consumer demands. Ultimately, the characteristics of the NPM, which have made it appealing and attractive outside the United States, have made it anathema to American public administrationists.

In their classic work *Postmodern Public Administration*, Miller and Fox (2006) explore postmodernism in the context of public administration. They deconstruct a number of orthodox concepts or theories in the field, such as the representative democratic accountability feedback loop model. Under this model of democracy, the authors point out, "*the people* are sovereign" and "policy reflects their wishes" (Miller and Fox 2006, 4; emphasis in the original). However, they go on to reason, this model "presupposes the empirical presence of the people," which is problematic, because "the phrase *the people* masks the radical absence of any such monistic aggregation, of any such consensus. Instead, there are multiple perspectives, multiple interests, and vast fields of conflict" (p. 5; emphasis in the original). They go on to question whether elected officials even act on behalf of "the people" and further challenge such enshrined concepts as *the* public interest.

Miller and Fox also deconstruct existing alternatives to orthodoxy, including constitutionalism. The call for constitutionalism has been made by many in the field of public administration, including Rosenbloom, Rohr, Bertelli, and Lynn, as discussed earlier in this chapter. According to this approach the U.S. Constitution and related laws legitimize and justify bureaucratic actions; that is to say, bureaucrats owe their loyalty and allegiance to the people via the Constitution and not to their elected political superiors. But Miller and Fox see constitutionalism as masked orthodoxy, unresponsive to the demands of postmodernism. The postmodern environment within which public administration must function, they argue, celebrates diversity and otherness. It supports the continual challenge to orthodoxy and universalism in favor of multiple and competing realities.

As an alternative to orthodoxy, Miller and Fox propose what they refer to as "discourse theory," which supports equal participation in policy dialogues. Interactive policy networks would become key, whereby multiple access points would exist, thus engendering greater authenticity to democratic theory. To say the least, their work encourages students of public administration—researchers and practitioners—to think outside the box.

SUMMARY

This chapter has illustrated the range of epistemic traditions based on qualitative methods for theory building in public administration; each represents a unique approach for the exploration and attainment of knowledge or truth. Certainly innumerable examples of research in public administration and management could be offered. Only a small sampling is provided here for illustrative purposes. Examples of quantitative approaches are presented in chapter 6.

NOTES

1. Some argue that qualitative methods tend to be more appropriate in the early stages of research (e.g., exploratory stage) and for theory building, whereas quantitative methods are more appropriate when theory is well developed and for the purpose of theory testing and refinement. This distinction is not made here. In addition, as Yin (2009) point outs, in practice, no research method is entirely quantitative or qualitative. Surveys, for example, may involve the collection of qualitative data relying on open-ended questions as well as quantitative data using closed questions.

2. See McNabb's (2004) schematic for research in political science.

3. Interpretivism and constructivism tend to be viewed as related, sometimes synonymous approaches. See, e.g., Denzin and Lincoln 2005. But compare with Yanow and Schwartz-Shea (2006b), who discuss the different and confusing uses of constructivism in such disciplines as sociology and psychology. Also see McNabb 2008.

4. Also see Yanow (1999), a book-length manuscript devoted to interpretive policy analysis.

5. Traditionally, hermeneutics involved the interpretation and analysis of religious texts or scriptures such as the Bible.

6. Also see, e.g., Rosenbloom 1975, 1977, 1978, 1983a, 1988b; and Rosenbloom and O'Leary 1996.

7. See the discussion of Rohr's work in Terry 2003.

8. Craig Thomas's work spans across a number of categories including interpretivism, positivism, and postpositivism. See Thomas 1997; Schweik and Thomas 2002.

9. Also see Franklin (2001), who analyzes interview transcripts of federal officials to determine agency reactions to the Government Performance and Results Act of 1993, and Riccucci et al. (2004), who examine the transcripts of caseworker-client interactions in their study of the role of public managers in the implementation of welfare reform.

10. See, e.g., the content analysis of case law around affirmative action in Kellough (2006).

11. Feminist theory is also examined from postmodernist approaches.

12. For a discussion of the application grounded theory in public administration research, see McNabb 2008. For examples of its use, see Durant 2007; Agranoff 2007; King, Feltey, and Susel 2001.

13. Ethnographic methods span other research traditions, e.g., postmodernism and even empiricism. It is also worth noting that, e.g., the grounded theory approach uses many of the techniques of ethnography—interviews, participant observation.

14. Also see, e.g., Selden, Sowa, and Sandfort 2006; Sandfort 2000, 2003.

15. For an ethnographic study that develops a model of bureaucratic politics, see Brower and Abolafia 1997.

16. See Nolan (2005), who points out that rationalists, despite their glorification of mathematics as their "model" methodology for arriving at the truth, believe that imagination plays a critical role in the attainment of mathematical knowledge.

17. Also see Meier 1993b.

18. Herbert Simon described management as a design science in his 1969 book *The Sciences of the Artificial*. Design science calls for the use of scientific principles, information technology, and even the imagination in defining or conceptualizing systems whose goals are to maximize efficiency. As an intellectual endeavor in public administration, the design sciences are virtually absent (but see note 19 below). Of course, if schools or departments of public administration or more likely, policy, have reconceptualized or repackaged design sciences as, let us say, decision support or science, or policy design, there continues to be some research activity, albeit relatively little in public administration. Design science is an approach that continues to prevail in such fields as engineering, business or organization studies, and information systems. See, e.g., Hodgkinson and Healey 2008; Mathieson 2007; March and Storey 2008; Adomavicius et al. 2008.

19. I am excluding here the work of such scholars as John Bryson, whose work does not fit precisely in the design sciences as conventionally defined. His work in the area of design and management (see, e.g., Bryson, Crosby, and Stone 2006) has been influential to public administrative theory.

20. Empiricism is a contested term among philosophers, including Locke, Berkeley, and Hume. Some draw distinctions between "classical" empiricism and twentieth-century empiricism. For a discussion, see Law 1993; Spicer 2006. It should also be noted that some confute empiricism with logical positivism. Also see Rosenberg (2008), who views Hume as a forerunner to the logical positivist movement.

21. Logical empiricism is also sometimes viewed as synonymous with logical or scientific positivism. For the purposes of this book only the terms logical positivism or simply positivism are used. See, e.g., Hardcastle 2005.

22. Narratives and storytelling have also been classified as interpretivist. See, e.g., Ospina and Dodge 2005; and for the use of war narratives, see Callahan, Dubnick, and Olshfski 2006.

23. See Bouckaert 2008; Ingraham 1995; Gormley 1996.

24. White (1999, 6) argues that all research is storytelling or narration in that any type of knowledge "is grounded in language and discourse and expressed in narrative form through conversations." Also see Maynard-Moody and Musheno 2006; Hummel 1991.

25. Also see Milward 1994, 1996; Milward, Provan, and Else 1993.

26. "Field" does not necessarily imply physical location; e.g., field studies can also involve telephone interviews.

27. For other examples, see Sandfort, Selden, and Sowa 2008; Riccucci 2005; Dicke 2002; Thurmaier and Willoughby 2001.

28. A case against the use of best practices is made in Weiss 1994.

29. See, e.g., Doig and Hargrove 1987; Behn 1991; Barzelay 1992; Denhardt 1993; Riccucci 1995; Denhardt and Denhardt 2001.

30. Rainey and Thompson's profile is part of an administrative profile series established by *Public Administration Review's* editor-in-chief, Richard Stillman, in 2006. For additional profiles of exemplars in that series, see Hutchinson and Condit 2009; Schachter 2008; Radin 2007; Cooper and Bryer 2007.

31. For scholars writing from the standpoints of education and social psychology, see, e.g., Clark and Creswell 2008; Reichardt and Rallis 1994; Tashakkori and Teddlie 1998. For a scholar writing from a perspective of experimental psychology, see Rosenthal 1976.

32. QCA, or qualitative comparative analysis, is a research technique used in such fields as political science, policy analysis, social work, and sociology that seeks to increase the total number of comparisons which can be made across cases.

33. Again, it is important to note that there is a degree of overlap between and among the various research traditions.

34. Also see Fischer 2000; deLeon 1990; Dryzek 1990; and Durning 1993, who offers four types of participatory policy analysis.

35. Clear-cutting refers to a process of felling or cutting down and removing trees from an entire tract of forest.

36. The analysts and researchers worked in state or local government agencies, universities, legislatures, or nonprofit advocacy organizations.

37. For examples of the use of Q methodology in the private sector, also see Van Exel and de Graaf 2005.

38. The agencies include the Port Authority of New York and New Jersey, the Newark District Office of the Immigration and Naturalization Service, and the township of Montclair, New Jersey.

39. Also see Brewer, Selden, and Facer 2000, who rely on Q methodology to examine perceptions about public service motivation.

40. For the earlier edition of their book, see Fox and Miller 1995.

41. Although it is beyond the scope of this book, many have pointed to the disutility of this concept. For a discussion, see, e.g., Myers 2002.

Theory Building through Quantitative Research

This chapter addresses theory building in public administration through the use of quantitative research. The two epistemic approaches included here are empiricism and logical positivism (see table 4.1). As was noted in chapter 5, this is not a textbook describing a step-by-step process for conducting quantitative research. Instead a number of examples of quantitative epistemic approaches are offered for illustrative purposes.

EMPIRICISM

Empirical studies can make use of qualitative methods, as presented in chapter 5; quantitative methods; or a combination of quantitative and qualitative analysis, sometimes referred to as triangulation or mixed methods, which are addressed in chapter 7. Examples of quantitative empirical studies can be seen in the plethora of descriptive studies in the field of public administration, such as those examining representative bureaucracy and related issues (see Chih-Wei and Winslow 2006; Guy and Newman 2004; Pynes 2000; Naff 1994; Guy 1993; Wise 1990; Rosenbloom 1977).[1] As was noted in chapters 4 and 5, representative bureaucracy is a normative theory maintaining that the social demographics of bureaucracy *ought* to reflect those of the general population it serves. Kingsley (1944), Mosher (1968), Frederickson (1971, 1980, 1990), Krislov (1974), Rosenbloom (1977), Krislov and Rosenbloom (1981), and Meier (1975) all greatly contributed to the development of this theoretical construct. Early descriptive studies tended to examine passive representativeness,[2] or the degree to which the social composition of the bureaucracy mirrored that of the general population.[3] For example, in a very early study Sigelman (1976) examined the representativeness of women in state and local government from 1970 to 1972.[4] He constructed a representation ratio as follows:

$$\text{Female representation } = \frac{\text{Female percentage of government employees}}{\text{Female percentage of working-age population}}$$

As he describes this formula, a ratio of 1.00 signifies perfect representation of women in state and local government workforces, based on their proportion of a state's working-age population. Anything lower than 1.00 suggests underrepresentation of women and above 1.00 indicates overrepresentation. His study found that in every state during that period, women were overrepresented in state and local government jobs. However, he also examined the job level at which women were employed through a stratification ratio:

$$\text{Female stratification } = \frac{\text{Female percentage of higher-level posts}}{\text{Female percentage of lower-level posts}}$$

His findings revealed that women were disproportionately found in lower-level positions in all states.

In a more recent study, Naff and Crum (2000) examined federal employment data from 1979 to 1996 to determine whether a U.S. president's views of affirmative action correlated with the representation of women and people of color in federal jobs. They present data on the percentage-point increase of women and people of color annually under each presidential administration as well as data on the percentage of career Senior Executive Service jobs—the highest level of career jobs in the federal government—held by women and people of color each year since 1979. On the basis of their analysis, they find little evidence of a correlation between presidential views and the representation of women and people of color in the federal service.

Another example of quantitative empiricism can be seen in Arsneault's case study of welfare reform in urban and rural communities in Kentucky.[5] Arsneault (2006) interviewed case managers in 120 counties to determine the challenges they face in implementing welfare reform. Through a host of descriptive statistics, she finds that "case managers . . . suggest that although some federal welfare guidelines, including maintenance of effort standards and broad goals of self-sufficiency, ought to be retained, many of the federal requirements associated with PRWORA [the Personal Responsibility and Work Opportunity Reconciliation Act of 1996; i.e., welfare reform] create standards not easily met, especially in rural America" (Arsneault 2006, 174).

In their study of federal, state, and local government human resources management practices and systems, Hays and Kearney (2001) provide quantitative empirical evidence showing that these practices and systems respond to environmental change as needed. Hays and Kearney administered a survey to 563 federal, state, and local government personnel directors, and to the entire 1998 ($N = 421$) membership of the American Society for Public Administration's Section on Personnel and Labor Relations. Their response rate was 295, or 108 from the section's members and 187 from personnel directors. Through the use of various descriptive statistics, they find that "technological innovations, changes in workplace expectations, new private-sector approaches, political pressures, reinventing government strategies, and other factors are expected to push some mainstream personnel techniques and activities toward the margins of the field. Position classification, paper-and-pencil exams, the rule of three, conventional performance appraisal techniques, and other procedures that are being used today are expected to decline substantially in importance during the next decade" (Hays and Kearney 2001, 594).

Kellough and Nigro's (2002) research reports on public employees' perceptions of Georgia's pay-for-performance plan. Their survey of about 3,000 state employees finds that workers have little confidence in the plan's ability to effectively measure and evaluate their performance and then link the outcomes to compensation. Notwithstanding these concerns, their findings show that, overall, employees are satisfied with their jobs, agencies, and situation working for the state of Georgia.

Rubin's (2007) study of the federal budget process shows that it has become fragmented, ad hoc, and unable to prioritize during the previous eight years.[6] She provides quantitative empirical evidence suggesting several reasons for the unraveling of federal budgets: "[One factor was] the mismatch between the budget process in 1998, which was designed to eliminate deficits, and the emerging budgetary surpluses of that time. A second contributing factor was the desire to reduce taxes while expenditures were increasing as a result of wars and natural disasters. The consequences of this great unraveling include the failure to fund Medicare and Social Security adequately when the opportunity was presented, as well as threats to constitutional and democratic governance. Renewed reform may require greater transparency and a willingness to embarrass elected officials with iconic stories" (Rubin 2007, 608).

The examples given above are but a few illustrations of quantitative empirical studies in public administration.[7] There are also a multitude of empirical studies that triangulate, using both qualitative and quantitative methods. These are presented in chapter 7. In short empirical studies can be qualitative, as seen in chapter 5; quantitative, as seen in this chapter; or a combination of both. Most important, empiricism should not be confused with positivism or logical positivism.[8] That is to say, empiricism, even in a quantitative form, does not share positivism's rigid verifiability criterion. There is a multitude of empirical studies in public administration, and to a certain degree, they dominate the research base in the field. But beginning most prominently in the late 1980s, with the "realization" of behaviorism in public administration or, more precisely, public management (see chapter 3), a substantial body of literature has been produced in the tradition of logical positivism.

LOGICAL POSITIVISM

As discussed in earlier chapters, logical positivism is a philosophic view holding that reality is attainable by empirically testing and *verifying* logically derived hypotheses. In this sense, knowledge of reality is driven by immutable, universal laws that are independent of the researcher. Positivist research is explanatory and nomothetic, in that it seeks to explain variations in phenomena, identifying and creating general or universal standards or laws. It is concerned with that which is predictable and general, as compared with say, interpretivism, which is ideographic and concerned with individual, specific, particular, and unique cases. Nomothetic research represents the search for abstract universal principles, whereas idiographic represents an effort to understand the meaning of contingent, accidental, and often subjective phenomena. Generally, nomothetic approaches are quantitative, and idiographic approaches are qualitative.

As recognized earlier, Herbert Simon was a driving force in the call for positivist research in public administration. Having been influenced by the behavioral movement in the social sciences, he argued for the use of "scientific" principles in the study of public administration. He stressed the importance of objectivity in research and maintained that experimentation is the best way to acquire knowledge. Interestingly, however, despite Simon's call for positivism—and the faction of scholars, especially from public policy schools, who sought to make public administration more positivistic, particularly through a public management incarnation—it was not until the 1980s and 1990s that the field began to see a definable mass of scholarship in the positivist tradition. And by the early part of the twenty-first century, it had burgeoned.[9]

One area of research where there have been numerous positivistic studies is representative bureaucracy. As was noted in chapter 4, Kenneth Meier has done a tremendous amount of work on this subject and has contributed greatly to the development of this theory. Early studies of representative bureaucracy were based on descriptive data and focused on passive representation. Later studies, pioneered in large part by Meier,[10] examined active representativeness and sought to determine if there was a linkage between passive and active representation; that is, if social characteristics predicted policy behaviors or outcomes (also see Saltzstein 1979, 1983).[11]

An important positivist study on representative bureaucracy that also contributes to feminist theory is Keiser and colleagues' (2002) examination of the circumstances under which passive representation leads to active representation for women. It is a baseline study on the existence of active representation for women. Specifically, Keiser and her colleagues ask if passive representation of women in the Texas educational system has an impact on the performance of women students. Their study is based on data from 607 Texas high schools from 1995 to 1998, and their unit of analysis is at the school rather than district level. Combining feminist and neoinstitutionalist theory, Keiser and her colleagues suggest that a critical antecedent for a linkage between passive and active representation is that the policy area be gendered. They argue that "the fluid nature of what counts as women's issues makes it difficult . . . to identify a priori the issues for which we expect to find representative bureaucracy for gender unless we more clearly specify the necessary conditions for an issue to become gendered. We argue that a policy area can become gendered (1) because the policy directly benefits women as a class, (2) because the gender of the bureaucrat changes the client–bureaucrat relationship, or (3) because the issue has been defined as a women's issue through the political process" (Keiser et al. 2002, 556).

Their hypotheses include:

♦ "active representation will occur only in bureaucracies dealing with policy issues that directly benefit women as a class, gendered policy issues, and issues where the bureaucrats' gender identification changes the client–bureaucrat relationship."
♦ "although mission is not a necessary condition, passive representation in terms of gender might be expected to lead to active representation when the leaders of the bureaucracy or the bureaucracy's historical mission focus on assisting women. Active representation will increase as passive representation increases in agencies with an

advocacy mission but will not be as strong in agencies lacking this advocacy mission."

♦ "more hierarchical and centralized organizations will be less likely to link passive and active representation."

♦ "as the number of women in supervisory positions increases, active representation will increase."

♦ "organizations with a critical mass of women will be more likely to allow for active representation." (Keiser et al. 2002, 556–57)

Because mathematics scores are a paramount gender issue in education, these scores serve as the key independent variable in their model. In addition, control variables—including organizational resources and the task difficulty the organization faces in educating students (e.g., they note that poor students tend to have greater educational difficulties)—are included in the model. Their analysis reveals in part that women math teachers are, in accordance with their hypothesis, positively associated with the math scores of young girls in grade 8 as well as on the exit exam. This study by Keiser and her colleagues, with its focus on gendered roles and institutions, greatly advances the body of knowledge concerned with representative bureaucracy, particularly for women.

Certainly, as with other epistemic traditions, numerous examples can be offered of logical positivist studies in public administration.[12] An additional example can be seen in Bretschneider's (1990) examination into the utility of public management information systems. Specifically he asks whether there are differences in the management of information systems between public and private organizations. He begins by pointing to differences between public and private management information systems. He contends for example, that "both public and private data processing organizations have personnel and financial activities reviewed by other groups within the agency or firm. Public organizations, though, face additional review by higher levels within the executive branch of government as well as legislative and advocacy groups. The effect of these additional layers of oversight is to make individuals and groups feel that they exert less control than comparable private sector managers over their various activities" (Bretschneider 1990, 537).

Bretschneider develops hypotheses about other significant environmental and managerial differences including the fact that, unlike private management information system managers, public management information system managers are at a lower hierarchical level, must contend with bureaucratic red tape, and must center their planning activities on extraorganizational, not internal linkages, thus making them more interdependent on other organizations.

Through a stratified sampling design, Bretschneider collects data from private organizations and state government agencies. His unit of analysis is the data-processing organization. He administered surveys to the two sampling frames: 1,361 state government data processing managers, and 1,395 in private organizations. He obtained usable data from 622 of the public-sector surveys and from 383 of those in the private sector. He ran several tests to determine that there were no selection biases.

To test his hypotheses that there are differences between public and private management information systems, Bretschneider included these control variables in his model: the size of the organization—measured by full-time equivalent staff—and the nature of computer technology (e.g., mainframe computers, microcomputers, or interactive minicomputers). Through an application of a standard linear model, using ordinary least squares estimation, he found that there were some statistically significant differences between public and private management information systems. For example, he reports that red tape created significantly longer delays for public systems compared with private systems. His results also support his hypothesis that public systems are much more interdependent than private systems. He also found significant differences in terms of planning as well, noting that public systems "made statistically significant less use of steering committees but significantly more use of formal planning processes tied to budgeting" (Bretschneider 1990, 541).

Bretschneider's research contributes greatly to public organization theory and behavior, particularly with respect to differences between public and private sector organizations. His study also advances our knowledge about the management of information systems—computer technology and data processing—by governments.

Another example of theory building through logical positivism can be seen in the research of Andrews, Boyne, and Walker (2006). They ask whether strategy content explains or predicts organizational performance in public organizations. Relying on earlier research, they conceptualize strategy content as having two components: strategic stance, or the general plan by which organizations maintain or improve their performance; and strategic actions, or the steps the organization takes to implement its plan. Their data were drawn from a survey of English local authorities (London boroughs, metropolitan boroughs, unitary authorities, and county councils). Their sample consisted of 386 authorities and 4,184 informants. On the basis of the available data and the response rate, their analysis was conducted on 1,245 informants or respondents and 119 local authorities.

The dependent variable in Andrews, Boyne, and Walker's model is a local authority's core service performance, which is calculated from an index of performance for English local authorities by the U.K. Audit Commission. The index classifies a local authority's performance as poor, weak, fair, good, or excellent. Strategy content, the leading independent variable, was constructed from survey responses, and measures were developed as follows:

- The local authority is at the forefront of innovative approaches.
- A major strategy for the authority is focusing on core business areas.
- Pressures from auditors and inspectors are key for driving performance improvement.
- Changes in services (e.g., providing new services to existing users).
- Seeking revenues (e.g., developing new ways to generate revenues).
- External organization (e.g., the local authority welcomes partnerships with private organizations).

The direction of the hypothesized relationships is axiomatic (e.g., an innovate authority is likely to be a higher performer rather than one that is not innovative; those focusing on core business areas are likely to be lower performers).

Other independent or control variables included the quantity and diversity of services. With respect to the former, Andrews, Boyne, and Walker hypothesized that organizations facing a demand for higher quantities of goods or services are less likely to provide an adequate quantity and quality of services per client. They further hypothesized that the more diverse the clientele (i.e., in terms of ethnicity), the more organizational performance would be constrained.

The results of their statistical model indicate that certain aspects of strategy content do positively affect organizational performance. For example, as they hypothesized, innovative local authorities are positively associated with organizational performance; and so, too, are those authorities that develop new markets for their services. Those authorities that continue to focus on existing, narrow routines, services, and clients will not perform as well. Andrews, Boyne, and Walker (2006, 58) conclude that their "evidence implies that public managers can make a significant difference in service standards through the strategies they follow." Their research advances the body of knowledge in public management and administration.

Willem and Buelens (2007) rely on structural equation modeling in their examination of knowledge sharing in public-sector organizations. They are particularly interested in explaining how coordination mechanisms developed by public organizations can affect knowledge sharing, which they define as "a process of exchanging and processing knowledge in a way that knowledge of one unit can be integrated and used in another unit" (Willem and Buelens 2007, 582). They develop a set of propositions to test the effects of organizationally driven cooperative mechanisms along with such factors as a worker's trust in other persons or parties. Through a questionnaire survey, they collected data from 358 Belgian public-sector workers across 90 different public-sector organizations or institutions, such as hospitals, schools, and the Flemish Education Department. Structural equation modeling pointed to the significance of lateral coordination by the government and of trust for knowledge sharing in Belgian public-sector organizations.

Another example of positivism in public administration can be found in Bozeman and Pandey's (2004) research on how decision content affects various aspects or processes of decision making in the areas of budget cutbacks and information technology. On the basis of existing research, they develop four hypotheses to test whether decision content affects: (1) Who participates in decision making, (2) the time required for decision making, (3) the decision criteria employed, and (4) the quality of information used in decision making and the amount of red tape. They administered a survey to 518 state-level managers across the 50 states and the District of Columbia involved in information management activities in health and human services agencies. They received a total of 274 responses.

Decision content was operationalized based on respondents' description of a major organizational decision occurring in the last year in which they had participated. A binary variable was then created for each of the two decision types—budget cutback and information technology—with 1 indicating the presence of relevant content and 0 indicating the absence of relevant content. Bozeman and Pandey point out that they relied on partial correlation rather than multiple regression because they were using several independent variables to determine their relationship on only two dependent variables.

Their results suggest that "decision content determines the subsequent process" (Bozeman and Pandey 2004, 562). They go on to say that this is due to the significant impact content has on decision criteria, information quality, red tape, and decision time and flow. Their findings further indicate that "information technology and budget cutback decisions differ in important ways. For information technology decisions, cost-effectiveness is not a significant criterion, average decision time is much longer, and decisions are generally viewed as permanent and stable. For cutback decisions, cost-effectiveness is a significant criterion, decisions are made much more quickly, and they are viewed as unstable and changeable. Surprisingly, decision content does not appear to affect the number of participants" (p. 553).

A final example of positivist research can be seen in Heinrich's (1999) examination of the effectiveness with which Job Training and Partnership Act (JTPA) administrators managed and implemented the use of a performance-based system to allocate funds to competing contractors for the delivery of employment services (e.g., job training) in Chicago from July 1984 through June 1993. The purpose of the JTPA was to help eligible participants find jobs, increase their earning power, and reduce their dependency on welfare. Through multiple and logistic regression analyses, Heinrich found that the local JTPA agency did rely on outcomes obtained from its performance-based system to allocate resources to local service providers. However, she also found that the performance system was poorly designed and that the performance measures were not correlated with the JTPA's program goals.

Obviously, myriad positivist studies could be highlighted as contributing to theory building. This chapter offers only a few examples. The following chapter offers examples of mixed methods, which is a hybrid of qualitative and quantitative approaches.

NOTES

1. Logical positivist studies of representative bureaucracy are presented later in this chapter.

2. Exceptions to this include Meier 1975 and Meier and Nigro 1976.

3. See, e.g., Nachmias and Rosenbloom 1973; Grabosky and Rosenbloom 1975; Thompson 1976; Rosenbloom and Featherstonhaugh 1977; Hale and Kelly 1989; Wise 1990.

4. For early descriptive studies on representative bureaucracy, also see, e.g., Kranz 1976; Krislov 1974; Krislov and Rosenbloom 1981.

5. For case studies relying on budget data, see, e.g., Hildreth 2009; Ho 2007.

6. For additional examples, see Hildreth and Miller 2002; Willoughby 2004.

THEORY BUILDING THROUGH QUANTITATIVE RESEARCH

7. Also see, e.g., Saxton, Guo, and Brown 2007; Newcomer 2007; Yang and Melitski 2007; Poister and Thomas 2007; Light 2006; Moynihan 2006; Elling and Thompson 2006; Cho 2004; Bowman 2004; Roberts 2004; Schneider and Jacoby 2003; O'Leary and Raines 2001; Agranoff and McGuire 1998; Furlong 1998; Shulock 1998; Golden 1998; Cigler 1994.

8. However, as noted in chapters 1 and 5, logical empiricism is sometimes used synonymously with logical positivism. This approach is not adopted here. For a discussion, see Hardcastle 2005.

9. Some may argue that the Public Management Research Association and its journal, the *Journal of Public Administration Research and Theory*, were driving forces here.

10. See, e.g., Meier 1975, 1993a, 1993b; Meier, Wrinkle, and Polinard 1999; Meier and Smith 1994; Meier and Stewart 1992; Meier, Stewart, and England 1989; Meier and Nigro 1976.

11. For additional representative bureaucracy studies in a logical positivist tradition other than those previously cited, see, e.g., Saidel and Loscocco 2005; Riccucci and Meyers 2004; Naff 2001; Dolan 2002; Selden 1997; Hindera 1993; Kellough 1990; Saltzstein 1979, 1983.

12. For illustrative purposes, also see Andrews 2008; Wood and Fan 2008; Van der Wal and Huberts 2008; Wright and Pandey 2008; Caruson and MacManus 2008; Ya Ni and Bretschneider 2007; Jang and Feiock 2007; Moynihan and Pandey 2007; Robinson and Meier 2006; Kim and Lee 2006; Anderson and Smirnova 2006; Fernandez and Smith 2005; Boyne et al. 2004; Moon and Bretschneider 2002; Kim 2002.

Theory Building through Mixed-Methods Research

The use of triangulation, or mixed methods, has become increasingly popular in public administration because it combines the benefits of qualitative and quantitative methods.[1] As was noted in chapter 4, this approach has been relied upon by empiricists as well as postpositivists, and it has also been relied upon *within* qualitative and quantitative traditions. Patton (2001, 306) points out that relying on "a combination of data types—triangulation . . . —increases validity as the strengths of one approach can compensate for the weaknesses of another approach." Similarly, Creswell (2009, 203) makes the point that "there is more insight to be gained from the combination of both qualitative and quantitative research than either form by itself. Their combined use provides an expanded understanding of research problems."

It should be noted that some have questioned the utility of mixed methods, given that this approach blends together the underlying assumptions of divergent epistemic traditions. For example, Tashakkori and Teddlie (2003, 94; emphasis in the original) ask whether the research approach can or should combine "the realist, objectivist, value-neutral perspectives *and* the constructivist, subjectivist, value-engaged perspectives." Their short answer is yes, in order to derive the strengths of the various approaches. Similarly, Yang, Zhang, and Holzer (2008) also argue that mixed methods are appropriate and should be relied upon for public administration research.[2] They first point out that some camps will continue to argue that the use of "quantitative and qualitative paradigms are incompatible due to their mutually exclusive epistemological and ontological assumptions. Therefore using different methods will lead to essentially different observations of the same phenomenon" (Yang, Zhang, and Holzer 2008, 38).

However, Yang, Zhang, and Holzer (2008, 38–39) further state that "[others] reject the dichotomy between the quantitative and the qualitative, attempting to integrate both methodologies for the same study. The quantitative and qualitative methods will support each other and enhance the credibility of the research. . . . We contend that qualitative and quantitative designs are complementary. Researchers can use a parallel strategy, simultaneously applying both designs." They conclude that "public administration may benefit greatly from more conscious efforts to apply multiple paradigms in a research project" (p. 39).

Triangulation, or mixed methods, becomes particularly important in applied fields in that it provides flexibility in efforts to find solutions to practical, real-world problems. Greene (2007, 65), for example, points out that mixed methods are critical for applied fields because the "work takes place in consequential sites of life and work." Similarly, Tashakkori and Teddlie (2003) argue that mixed methods are critical "where practical decisions stress the utility of multiple data sources for decision-making purposes." They go on to say that applied fields "often require multiple methods to understand complex social phenomena" (p. 679). Moreover, as Greene (2007) concludes, mixed methods serve as a "rapprochement" between the demands or desires for qualitative and quantitative approaches, and are very appropriate for social inquiry.

There has also been a growing movement in political science toward the use of mixed methods. Elman (2008, 273) points out that "the American Political Science Association's (APSA) organized section on Qualitative and Multi-Method Research . . . is now the third largest of the APSA's 37 sections." He calls for the "multiple-logics-of-inference view," noting that "pluralism within the field has been exhibited in the increasingly sophisticated use of multiple methods in composite research designs, through nesting, iteration and other strategies" (p. 272).

In 2007 a new periodical, the *Journal of Mixed Methods Research*, was launched to promote research relying on mixed methods. In its maiden issue, prominent scholars of mixed-method research, Tashakkori and Creswell (2007, 3) pointed out that the journal "starts a new era in the conceptualization and utilization of integrated approaches across the social and behavioral sciences. For almost three decades, various scholars have discussed and debated the concepts, methods, and standards of quality for studies that utilize a combination of qualitative and quantitative approaches. . . . Evolving from these discussions has been a body of literature devoted to issues of worldview, nomenclature, typology, design, analysis, and evaluation of mixed methods studies."

EXAMPLES OF MIXED-METHODS RESEARCH IN PUBLIC ADMINISTRATION

A number of studies in public administration have made use of mixed methods. Jodi Sandfort, for example, has relied extensively on field studies in her research on social welfare and has relied on a mixture of qualitative and quantitative methods. In one study, she and her colleagues examine whether the various tools governments employ to implement social policy have an impact on organizational performance (see Sandfort, Selden, and Sowa 2008). In their field-based study of twenty-two organizations, they examine how three difference public policy tools—grants, contracts, and vouchers—can affect the performance of organizations providing childhood care and education services. They specifically ask: "Does the receipt of various government tools have differential impacts on measures of organizational effectiveness?" (p. 413). Their field study of twenty-two agencies in the states of New York and Virginia involved site visits, interviews with managers as well as teachers and parents, and an examination of agency documents. Their qualitative data revealed that the different tools have a distinct impact on, for instance, financial management practices. Organization staff needed to modify their behaviors for documenting costs or developing payment schedules based on whether grants, contracts, or vouchers were used. They found that the type of policy tool employed also affected program capacity. Head Start grants, for example, stipulate performance standards on child development practices for classrooms and community engagement techniques, which in turn require agencies to make programmatic changes to meet those standards.

Sandfort and her colleagues then rely on quantitative data to further explore the relationship between government tools and organizational performance. Their quantitative model sought to determine the statistical relationship between the use of grants (Head Start), contracts (prekindergarten) and vouchers (Department of Social Services), and organizational performance. They point out that there is no consensus among researchers on how to best conceptualize organizational effectiveness. They thus rely on a model they developed for previous research (see Sowa, Selden, and Sandfort 2004). The quantitative model, too, indicates that the different implementation tools employed by government organizations have different affects on agency performance in delivering services. In particular, their findings suggest that grants have the most significant, positive effects on organizational effectiveness.

Herzog (1993) also relies on triangulation in his examination of an organizational doctrine he refers to as "practitioner-held" theory. This theory or model represents the knowledge that practitioners gain from the use of qualitative and quantitative methods, which leads to a set of generalities or theoretical dimensions that shape normative positions of practitioners on organizational matters. These positions ultimately assist practitioners in their behaviors. As Herzog maintains (1993, 447): "These positions are believed to inform, dictate, and constrain the actions of practitioners, and these perceptions may have emerged as a result of past action–consequence relationships. In either sequence, the practitioners' positions are grounded in limited instrumental rationality."

To both develop and determine the applicability and value of practitioner-held theory, Herzog combines the use of qualitative methods (i.e., interviews with city managers) with quantitative methods (i.e., a survey of city managers). His sample included 220 city managers, and based on the results of his interviews and survey, he developed ten theoretical dimensions of organizational behavior: structural reform or reorganization, task management or specialization, insular governance, participative management, Theory Y, norm setting, participatory democracy, citizen input into decision making, community leadership, and legislative involvement in management.

Herzog created a scale to map out practitioners' responses to the relative importance of the ten theoretical dimensions. Possible scores for each dimension ranged from 3 to 15, where 3 represents the maximum practitioner support and 15 represents maximum practitioner opposition. Herzog (1993, 436) points out that lower "means (3 to 7.5) show practitioner support for the theoretical dimension, higher scores (10.5 to 15) show practitioner opposition for the theoretical dimensions, and midrange scores (7.6 to 10.4) suggest practitioner inconclusiveness for the theoretical dimension." His findings indicate that the qualitative results of his study did not always match or correspond with the quantitative data. For example, on the dimension of structural reform, the quantitative findings suggest that city managers do not support restructuring or reorganizing as a technique for improving decision making or increasing efficiency and effectiveness. Yet his interview data suggest that restructuring is an important dimension for city managers and, hence, practitioner-held theory. On the dimension of participative management, the quantitative findings illustrate that managers support it, while the qualitative data were more nuanced and ambiguous or qualified. For instance, some managers were more supportive of participative management in theory but not practice. An important point that needs to be made here is that although triangulation is intended to strengthen the overall value of research, it can sometimes lead to contradictory findings where the qualitative and quantitative data are at odds with one another.

Pollitt and Bouckaert (2004) also combine the use of qualitative and quantitative methods in their insightful book *Public Management Reform: A Comparative Perspective*, a rare cross-national and international analysis of public management reform. Their research examines the multitude of management reforms to ten countries that belong to the Organization for Economic Cooperation and Development: Australia, Canada, Finland, France, Germany, the Netherlands, New Zealand, Sweden, the United Kingdom, and the United States. They provide key features or strategies of public management reform, such as budget cuts, efforts to eliminate waste, the modernization of administrative systems through use of private-sector management practices, the application of market-type instruments, and increased reliance on privatization or contracting out. These strategies are much like those proposed by the new public management (NPM), as discussed in chapter 3. They use these elements as a template for analyzing the various public management reforms implemented by the ten countries.

Interestingly, they find through qualitative and quantitative empirical data that the various management reforms to these countries have not necessarily embraced a NPM framework, as proponents of that movement would have us believe. Pollitt and Bouckaert (2004) instead find that, though some countries like New Zealand, the United States, and the United Kingdom have adopted NPM reforms, others such as France and Germany have staved off market-type reforms and privatization. They also find that "it is not simply a case of some countries being reluctant or opposed to the NPM; it is more the case that there are alternatives and positive concepts of modernization, one of which we describe as the 'New Weberian State'" (p. 3). Eschewing the traditional, negative views of Weberian bureaucracy, Pollitt and Bouckaert (2004, 62) argue that the new Weberian state includes such positive values as "continuity, honesty, and a high commitment to equity in dealing with the citizen-public." Last, they maintain that the variations in adopted reforms have more to do with the politico-administrative systems of each country than prevailing economic forces or the "relational affinities and obligations of civil society" (Pollitt and Bouckaert 2004, 13; also see their discussion on pp. 63–64).

Another example of research that combines qualitative and quantitative approaches can be seen in Goodsell's classic *The Case for Bureaucracy*.[3] Through case studies and various statistical analyses, Goodsell (2004) illustrates that, contrary to popular belief, government bureaucracies are not all grossly inefficient, wasteful, and incompetent. For example, relying on secondary data, he evaluates a host of citizen satisfaction surveys on government at various levels to show how favorable citizens' opinions are toward their governments. Throughout his study, he empirically demonstrates that "governmental administration in America, despite conventional opinion to the contrary, is relatively effective, reasonably efficient, and supportive of our democratic way of life" (Goodsell 2004, 139). He goes on to say: "While waste, incompetence, and corruption will always exist in government—and in all organizational sectors, for that matter—in the United States these problems are far less common and significant than we commonly believe. . . . As a consequence, I seize the popular synonym for bad government, "bureaucracy," and redefine it as a general social asset for the society" (p. 139).

Soss (1999) relies on triangulation in his examination of whether the designs of welfare programs affect clients' beliefs about their efficacy in asserting themselves in client–worker interactions, and ultimately about their political engagement overall. He states that because "clients associate the agency with government as a whole, these program-specific beliefs, in turn, become the basis for broader orientations toward government and political action" (Soss 1999, 364). He points to his "triangulation" of data sources from (1) in-depth interviews with fifty clients of Aid to Families with Dependent Children (AFDC)—now Temporary Assistance for Needy Families—and the social insurance program, Social Security Disability Insurance (SSDI), in a midsized Midwestern city; (2) ethnographic fieldwork at homeless shelters serving AFDC families and with disability support groups for SSDI recipients; (3) direct observation of clients' experiences with the welfare agency; and (4) survey data from the 1992 National Election Studies (NES) survey.

Soss finds that clients in both programs have views and make inferences about government in general based on their experiences with welfare agencies. In addition, at least for the AFDC cohort, clients believe that it is useless to challenge the welfare agency and that their political action in general would be ineffective. However, in his multivariate analysis of the NES data, which controlled for client background and allowed for the testing of his interview findings with a larger sample, he found that higher income, educational level, and stronger feelings of partisanship had a significantly positive effect on beliefs of external political efficacy. No significant relationships based on gender or race were found.

Although less popular, triangulation within qualitative or quantitative approaches has also been relied upon in public administration. An example of triangulation in a postpositivist tradition using solely qualitative methods can be seen in Lee's (2006b) *Institutionalizing Congress and the presidency: The U.S. Bureau of Efficiency, 1916–1933* (also see Lee 2006a).[4]

Lee's case study relied on three sources for triangulation: archival documents, news coverage, and published government documents. Lee explains that he became interested in the Bureau of Efficiency (BOE) while conducting a study on Franklin D. Roosevelt's Office of Government Reports. He had never heard of the BOE and indeed thought the name was a joke; really, he asked, could there be a "federal agency dedicated to efficiency in Washington?" (Lee 2006b, ix). He learned that the BOE was actually created in 1916 and that its mission was "to provide a small force of specialists to serve the President and the various administrative heads by studying specific problems of organization and business methods and developing constructive recommendations for improvement, and to provide information or recommendations on administrative and legislative matters" (Lee 2006b, ix). He was thus motivated to study the creation, existence, and abolishment of this relatively obscure BOE.

Lee poured over papers, transcripts, government documents, and other relevant archival materials at, for example, the Hoover Presidential Library; the Roosevelt Presidential Library; the National Archives in College Park, Maryland; the Center for Legislative Archives; the U.S. Senate Library; the Library of Congress; and the library of the Federal Trade Commission. In addition, he examined contemporaneous newspaper articles from the *New York Times, Washington Post, Wall Street Journal, Los Angeles Times*, and *Chicago Tribune*. Through triangulation, he weaves together a fascinating case study of how the BOE, operating as a Progressive Era reform agency, sought to promote such scientific management principles as efficiency and one best way. The BOE was the first central staff agency in the executive branch of the president, and through management and policy analyses, it was dedicated to assisting the president perform his job. The BOE, Lee (2006b, 3) found, was the "focal point of leadership and power in the federal government."

Lee also corrects a number of mischaracterizations of why the BOE was abolished. First, he points out that, contrary to leading academic accounts, the functions and staff of the BOE were never transferred to the Bureau of the Budget (BOB, the predecessor of the Office of Management and Budget); only the files and furniture of the BOE were transferred. Moreover, President Hoover did not abolish the BOE as a retrenchment move; Congress abolished it for political reasons—the agency's reports and recommendations to promote efficiency and reduce staffing continually threatened pet projects of senators and representatives. Arguing that the BOE duplicated the functions of the BOB, Congress voted to abolish the BOE in 1933 (see Lee 2003).

SUMMARY

In sum, the use of mixed methods has grown in popularity in public administration as well as other social science disciplines, and a number of scholars advocate this approach. As Yin (2009, 63) points out, "Mixed methods research can permit investigators to address more complicated research questions and collect a richer and stronger array of evidence than can be accomplished by any single method alone." Moreover, as Tashakkori and Creswell (2007, 4) point out, mixed methods research is still evolving and "developing and will do so for years to come. There are important unresolved issues, and unexplored aspects that need to be explored, in addition to the core issue of defining the nature of mixed methods research." Public administrationists as well as other social scientists are thus presented with opportunities to participate in the ongoing dialogues about the contours of mixed methods and their significance for the social and behavioral sciences.

NOTES

1. The concepts "triangulation" and "mixed methods" are used interchangeably here. Also, pragmatism is a philosophical position associated with mixed methods. For a discussion of the link, see, e.g., Tashakkori and Teddlie 2003. For a comprehensive treatment of mixed methods, see Tashakkori and Teddlie 2003; Clark and Creswell 2008.

2. Also see Greene 2007.

3. Also see Howell-Moroney (2008), who relies on mixed methods to study growth management policy.

4. For additional examples, see Lejano 2008; Drori and Weizmann 2007; Rockloff and Moore 2006; Torres 2004.

Heterogeneity in Epistemic Traditions

This book has examined the field of public administration through the lenses of the philosophy of science. It has offered evidence of a variety of epistemic traditions relevant to and valid for public administration research. Each tradition offers a unique contribution to theory building and testing in the field. Some rely on qualitative approaches, whereas others rely on quantitative or a combination of the both. As presented here, one is not necessarily better than the other; value choices are required, which are driven by the research questions, as is discussed further below. Moreover, the rich body of research that has been produced in public administration since its self-conscious inception can be "pure" or basic, whereby research is conducted for the sake of research and the acquisition of knowledge, even if it has no practical value. Or it can be applied research, whereby it does have some practical, applicable utility. Each type of research has been and will continue to be equally important to the development of the field. As has been noted, a one-size-fits-all approach to inquiry is not viable for public administration.

Rosenbloom (1983b), writing more than twenty-five years ago, argued that public administration from the standpoint of substance or "matter" is driven by dissimilar, competing values—managerial, political, and legal. As has been seen in this book, many scholars and practitioners would like to claim that public administration is driven by, or *ought* to be driven by, only one set of values (e.g., some maintain that it should be law, while others argue for management). But as Rosenbloom shows, each of the values, although divergent, contributes uniquely to public administration. And one set of values cannot and should not be permitted to drive out the others. Thus a critical and invaluable characteristic of our field, which marks it so distinctively, is its diversity or heterogeneity.

An analogy can be made with respect to the logic of inquiry in public administration. As with all the other social sciences, disagreements over questions of epistemology and methodology will never be resolved in public administration. Some will always be predisposed to logical positivism and its quantitative, explanatory techniques. Others will lean toward other approaches or even espouse the virtues of epistemic heterogeneity. This book has taken the latter position, arguing that no single philosophic approach can dominate or drive out the others. In fact, in the spirit of Rosenbloom's thesis or proposition, the different approaches to studying public administration have served to strengthen the field, ensuring that research is carried out in all traditions.

A SYNOPSIS OF THE EPISTEMIC TRADITIONS IN PUBLIC ADMINISTRATION

Table 8.1 provides a summary and examples of research approaches in public administration as they have been presented in this book. There may be some redundancy here, but for a topic as dense as the logic of inquiry, it may serve to foster a better understanding of the philosophies of science in public administration. It should also be noted that with respect to the contemporary thinkers listed in table 8.1, the categories are not mutually exclusive and my purpose is not to pigeonhole philosophers into a single epistemic tradition. Many of the scholars listed have written in a number of traditions. For example, Larry Lynn has written in the interpretivist tradition (e.g., his interpretations of the U.S. Constitution) and in the positivist tradition (e.g., his studies of governance and public management). Thus the assignment of scholars to a particular tradition is only illustrative of certain streams of their research.

As table 8.1 shows, the acquisition of knowledge in public administration is distinguished by the epistemic tradition, which drives the methods and recording techniques of the research. For example, interpretivists acquire knowledge through interpretations of the mind. Their culture, experiences, and worldviews cannot be divorced from their construction of reality. And, as discussed previously in this book, interpretivism emerged as a challenge to the positivist approach for studying and understanding human and social behavior. Interpretivists maintain that human and social behaviors are best understood by studying the ideas, thoughts, and views of the people being studied. Moreover, for interpretivists, the values and experiences of the researcher matter when the ideas of people or the written word are interpreted. Thus knowledge is based on the truth or reality as the interpretivist intended it to be. As Willis (2007, 6) points out: "Humans

Table 8.1 Summary and Examples of Epistemic Approaches to the Study of Public Administration

	Interpretivism (Antipositivism)	Rationalism	Empiricism	Positivism	Postpositivism	Post modernism/ Critical Theory
Philosophy of knowledge	Knowledge is derived from interpretations via the mind	Knowledge is acquired through reason	Knowledge is acquired through the senses	Knowledge is acquired through empirical testing and verification of hypotheses	Knowledge is acquired through conjecture and subject to falsification	Knowledge is acquired through social construction
Examples	Interpretation of texts (e.g., government documents; statutory law) to determine meaning behind written word	Normative discourse on, for example, the role of constitutional law in public administration	Descriptive studies of concentration of women in government	Experimental studies testing effects of managerial practices on street-level bureaucratic behavior	The use of Q-methods to determine the degree to which public values are reflected in public policies	Critical analysis and deconstruction of mainstream concepts, e.g., democratic accountability
	Content analysis of recorded transcripts of government officials	Conceptual analysis of the scope or meaning of public administration	Use of storytelling to derive insights on behaviors of frontline bureaucrats	Regression analysis explaining potential differences between public and private management information systems	Use of mixed methods to determine whether use of contracts affects organizational performance	Critical analysis of nature of politics and its implications for a scientific approach to governance
	Use of ethnography to examine internal workings of a public organization	Metaethical analysis of the moral responsibilities of public administrators	Best practices of government officials or organizations	Structural equation modeling testing if gender helps explain pay in government jobs	Use of mixed methods to examine public management reforms globally	Feminist discourse on gender roles in public administration
Recording technique	Qualitative	Qualitative	Qualitative and quantitative	Quantitative	Qualitative and quantitative	Qualitative
Methods	Ethnography; action research; descriptive case studies; content and narrative analysis	Conceptual analyses; normative discourse; metaethical inquiry	Case studies; field studies; storytelling; narratives; best practices	Field studies; experimental research; opinion research	Ethnography; narratives; storytelling; case studies of Participatory Policy Analysis; Q methodology	Literary criticism; historical essays; dialectical analysis; field research; discourse analysis; case studies
Contemporary philosophers and thinkers	Agranoff, Carroll, Phillip Cooper, Durant, O'Leary, Radin, Rohr, Stillman, West, Rice	Adams, Balfour, deLeon, Dubnick, Frederickson, Krislov, Lynn, Rosenbloom, Menzel	Behn, Brudney, Terry Cooper, Condrey, Denhardts, Holzer, Kearney, Lipsky, Maynard-Moody, Milward, Provan, Naff,	Boyne, Bozeman, Bretschneider, Brewer, Heinrich, Keiser, Kellough, Meier, O'Toole, Selden, Pandey	Bouckaert, Durning, Goodsell, Guy, Ingraham, Riccucci, Romzek, Sandfort, Thomas	Box, Fischer, Fox, Hummel, Hutchinson, McSwite, Miller, Raadschelders, Spicer, Stivers, Wamsley, White, Yanow

are . . . influenced by their subjective perception of their environment—their subjective realities. . . . If we are to fully understand the behavior of an 18-year-old delinquent, we must understand her view of the world around her. We must also understand the subjective perceptions of her by others in her social and cultural context. Thus, for interpretivists, what the world means to the person or group being studied is critically important to good research in the social sciences."

As table 8.1 further illustrates, interpretivists rely on such research tools and techniques as case studies, content analysis, and ethnography. Their research, as depicted throughout this book, is based in qualitative methods.

Rationalists acquire knowledge through reason, not experience or sense perception. Moreover, for them, knowledge is innate (i.e., present from birth) and based on intuition. Rationalism is based on the belief that reason and intellect are better tools for the construction of truth and reality than sense perception or experience. Spicer (1995, 14) describes rationalism in this fashion:

> The rationalist worldview sees men and women, potentially at least, as possessing substantial powers of reason and able to use that reason intentionally to improve outcomes for humanity. . . . Human problems of misery, poverty, and violence arise, according to rationalists, because of our collective failure to properly exercise our reason. The key to economic, political, and social improvement for the rationalist is the conscious application of human reasons. Reason can and should be used to provide the basis for a blueprint for a better human order.

Rationalists rely on qualitative research methods to examine a variety of topics in public administration, as indicated in table 8.1. For rationalists a better understanding of society, politics, and the government—its processes, behavior, and scope—can be acquired through reason and intuition.

Empiricism calls for knowledge acquisition and hence theory building via the senses or experiences. A critical reaction to rationalism, empiricists maintain that reason alone cannot build knowledge, but rather the basis of reality is observation. As McNabb (2004, 15–16; emphasis in the original) points out: "Empiricism means that all knowledge must be *sensed* to be real; faith alone—knowing that it is true because you believe it to be so—is an insufficient basis . . . as a foundation for knowledge." Empirical research can be qualitative or quantitative. For example, as seen in table 8.1, studies on the concentration of women in government may rely on descriptive statistics, and hence be classified as quantitative empiricism. Or case studies reporting in greater depth on the experiences of women in government may represent qualitative empiricism.

Positivism, or logical positivism, grew out of the behavioral movement in the social sciences and was championed in public administration by Herbert Simon. As has been noted, this philosophical movement was first known first as positivism, as advanced by Auguste Comte, and later as logical positivism, as advanced by the Vienna Circle, a group of philosophers, mathematicians, sociologists, physicists, and economists gathering in the Austrian capital in the early twentieth century promoting a new method, based on logical analysis, for the advancement of knowledge. As McGrath (2001, 231; emphasis in the original) points out,

> There was considerable divergence between many of the thinkers of the Circle, and . . . the views of some of its leading members would change as time progressed. . . . However, in very general terms it may be stated that one of the most fundamental themes of the group was that *beliefs must be justified on the basis of experience*. . . . The members of the group tended to place a particularly high estimation on the methods and norms of the natural sciences (which were seen as the most empirical of human disciplines) and a correspondingly low estimation on metaphysics (which was seen as an attempt to disengage with experience). Indeed, one of the more significant achievements of the Vienna Circle was to cause the word 'metaphysics' to have strongly negative connotations.

As has been discussed in this book, positivists hold that research on public administration must be driven by logically derived hypotheses that are tested and verified with such methods as regression analysis in its various forms (e.g., ordinary least squares, probit). A multitude of work has been conducted in this tradition, and it has greatly advanced theory building for the field.

Postpositivism, as has been noted, accepts the existence of error in research and considers the results or findings as probable until falsified. For postpositivists, "reality can never be fully apprehended, only approximated" (Denzin and Lincoln 2005, 11). Creswell (2009, 7) explains that "postpositivists challenge the traditional notion of the absolute truth of knowledge, . . . recognizing that we cannot be 'positive' about our claims of knowledge when studying the behavior and actions of humans. . . . Postpositivists hold a deterministic philosophy in which causes probably determine effects and outcomes."

Postpositivism can rely on qualitative, quantitative, and mixed methods, the latter of which has grown in popularity, particularly in applied fields such as public administration. As Denzin and Lincoln (2005, 11) point out, "Postpositivism relies on multiple methods as a way of capturing as much of reality as possible."

Postmodernism challenges conventional approaches to thinking and knowledge acquisition. It holds that because reality is a cultural and social construction, absolute or universal truths are unattainable. Denhardt and Denhardt (2007, 41; emphasis in the original) make this observation:

> While postmodernism is extremely complex and diverse, most postmodernists would argue that a problem we face today is that we have lost the capacity to tell what is *real*. All those previously held "world-views," as well as "scientific explanations" that seemed to work in the past, have been revealed to have fatal flaws, most of these related to the fact that these explanations were the products of particular places and particular times and could only address the world from the that largely unique standpoints. If we created the world through our language and our interactions, then there will inevitably be limitations on what we can claim to be "real."

Postmodernism holds that social and human behaviors cannot be reduced to measurable facts nor separated from values. Postmodernists question the "foundations" of public administration, arguing that these very foundations that have been held to be true are in actuality built on faulty, incomplete, imperfect, and unidimensional information, interpretations, beliefs, and observations. As is noted in table 8.1, postmodernists rely on a host of qualitative methods, including literary criticism, historical essays, and dialectical analyses.

LET RESEARCH QUESTIONS GUIDE THE CHOICE OF EPISTEMIC APPROACH

Jay White (1999, 184) has argued that

> there are many approaches to the study of public administration. . . . No one approach should be considered superior to another. The nature of the research question at hand should guide the selection of an approach, along with its attendant methods and techniques. If the research question asks for an explanation of why things have occurred in the way that they have and a prediction of how things might occur in the future, given certain events or interventions, explanatory research is called for. If the research question simply asks about what is going on here, interpretive research is called for.

> If we are suffering from an ideological, psychological, or historical obfusca-
> tion of the actual reality that is facing us, critical research is appropriate.
> Whatever question we face, we must properly align an approach that will
> address the question most appropriately.

Although White relies on a different taxonomy of epistemic traditions than the one used in this book, he nonetheless offered propositions similar to the ones advanced here.

Moreover, as many have argued, values and biases inevitably shape research questions. As Behn (1996, 92) has said, "Although the choice of a research question may be personal or even arbitrary, it is not without consequence. For this choice predetermines, in many ways, the strategy of research."

The key is that there are many viable and appropriate research traditions in public administration; the choice depends upon the questions asked and the answers sought. For example, if one is concerned with learning more about the contours and specifics of U.S. Supreme Court rulings around affirmative action, then an interpretive or rationalist approach might be best. As was noted in chapter 4, Naff (2001), in part, relies on an examina-tion of case law in her research on affirmative action in government set-tings. So, too, do Kellough (2006) and a number of others.[1] Conversely, if one is interested in discovering the effects of affirmative action rulings on, say, hiring and promotion decisions or the careers of people of color, one could take an empirical approach (e.g., single or multiple case studies of a given jurisdiction; field studies or best practices) or a positivist explanatory approach, whereby one or more of the independent variables in a multiple regression model will seek to explain the impact of court rulings or deci-sions on a dependent variable such as the hiring of women or people of color in local government jobs.

For example, McCrary (2007) examined the impact of court decisions on the hiring patterns of African Americans in police departments. The first part of his study relied on descriptive statistics to determine if court orders covering Chicago police departments increased the representation of African American police officers in the 1960s and 1970s. His findings showed that they did. In the second part of his study, through an explana-tory design, he relied on data from 314 large cities across the country to ask about the effects of court orders from 1960 to 1999 on police departments' decisions to hire African American police officers. Among several other variables (e.g., region, city demographics, city crime rates), he found that court orders did affect the hiring of African Americans by police depart-ments throughout the United States during that period.

Bremer and Howe (1988) relied on a best practice case study of how government agencies in Oregon were successful in promoting women to managerial positions. Through in-depth interviews with top managers, personnel directors, and successfully promoted women managers in seven local, state, and federal agencies in Oregon, they found that the strategies that proved most effective included developing goals and timetables in accordance with statutory or common law; a commitment to the upward mobility of women; and the aggressive recruitment of qualified women and providing training and career development for women.

Long (2007) has relied on a positivist, explanatory approach in his research seeking to determine whether the elimination of affirmative action by public universities has resulted in lower representations of people of color in universities. Relying on times-series analyses of public policies and court rulings on affirmative action, and then regression models, he finds evidence that the enrollment of people of color in universities has declined as a result of the elimination of affirmative action programs by the courts, administratively based policies, or voter referenda.

Slack (1987) asked the question, What explains city managers' support for the use of affirmative action in recruiting women to city jobs? On the basis of 290 questionnaires administered to city managers throughout the United States in 1985, Slack's regression analysis showed that certain background characteristics helped explain city managers' support for affirmative action; older, politically conservative city managers were less likely than younger, more liberal city managers to support the use of affirmative action. He also found that legal environment (e.g., court decisions and legal mandates) had a negative effect on managers' support for affirmative action. He reasoned that city managers could have resented the imposition of hiring targets and timetables set by law or court rulings. Conversely, community and city government demographics along with city managers' perceptions of local politics had a minimal or no effect on their support for affirmative action in the recruitment of women.

Similarly, an examination of the plethora of research on networks and network management indicates that several approaches have been relied upon to advance our knowledge in this area. Robert Agranoff, a pioneer in the study of networks, has produced a body of research on network management that has greatly advanced the field. His studies (e.g., Agranoff 1990, 2001, 2003, 2007), along with those conducted with McGuire (e.g., Agranoff and McGuire 1998, 2001a, 2001b, 2003), have been interpretive and empirical, with a reliance on grounded theory, case studies, survey research, descriptive statistics, and content and normative analyses.

Others in the field have studied network management from a positivist perspective. The body of research generated by Meier and O'Toole is the most prominent. Their explanatory studies (e.g., Meier and O'Toole 2001, 2002, 2003; O'Toole and Meier 2004a, 2004b) have addressed such questions and issues as the impact of networks on organizational performance and the effect of network management on policy implementation. A number of others have studied various aspects of network management in a positivist tradition (see, e.g., Huang and Provan 2007; Provan, Huang, and Milward, 2009; Percival, 2009; Krueathep, Riccucci, and Suwanmala, 2010). They have tested hypotheses such as the following:

♦ "The relationship between network embeddedness and trustworthi-ness is likely to strengthen as the network matures" (Provan, Huang, and Milward 2009).
♦ "Provider organizations that are more structurally embedded in a network will have a higher reputation as reported by other network members" (Provan, Huang, and Milward 2009).
♦ "Provider organizations that are more structurally embedded in a network will have a greater influence among network members" (Provan, Huang, and Milward 2009).
♦ "School system output is higher if superintendents exert manage-ment effort in networks surrounding them" (Meier and O'Toole 2001, 279).
♦ "To the extent that environmental shocks challenge or threaten pro-gram performance, network managers can be expected to protect the core performance bureaucracy from these forces" (Meier and O'Toole 2001, 279).

Again, as with other substantive issues in public administration, the purpose of the research and its concomitant questions drive decisions about which research approach is most suitable for studying network management.

Certainly, however, some may be so hardened in their views about the value of certain research traditions that they will remain intolerant of any form of epistemic heterogeneity. This book was not intended to resolve such intransigence. If Plato could not resolve it, no one can.

Instead, an important purpose of this book is to promote greater toler-ance of the diversity in research traditions, because the persistence of a single or specific research tradition has been detrimental to theory building in public administration. As Bozeman (2007) pointed out, allowing a desire for quantitative empirical evidence to drive research agendas thwarts the advancement of theory and knowledge in critical areas in the field. Perhaps Raadschelders (2005, 597) sums it up best: "The complexity of reality cannot be grasped through one approach (e.g., theory or method) only, given the human inclination to perceive the same 'thing' differently. We cannot but live with multiple approaches. . . . The selection of a research instrument (i.e., theory or method) must fit the material object (e.g., a policy, an organization, a budget) under investigation. Given many material objects (within the overall material object of government), this inevitably generates multiple techniques and instruments."

Future generations of public administrationists will generate, build, and test theories relevant to the field. A host of research traditions can be tapped; the choice will depend upon the purpose of the research and the questions asked. More informed choices could be made, to the extent that future scholars are well versed in all the applicable epistemic traditions. The challenge will be to ensure that students of public administration are being prepared in not only quantitative research approaches but also qualitative ones. Good, sound qualitative research is contingent upon whether scholars are adequately trained in the techniques, tools, and underlying philosophies associated with this type of research. Theoretical achievements and progress in the field of public administration, in effect, rest in the heterogeneity of research traditions.

NOTE

1. See Bradbury 2008; Riccucci 2007b; Naylor and Rosenbloom 2004; Rice and Mongkuo 1998; Nalbandian 1989; and the myriad articles appearing in law journals.

REFERENCES

Abolafia, Mitchel Y. 1996. *Making markets: Opportunism and restraint on Wall Street.* Cambridge, MA: Harvard University Press.

Adams, Guy B. 1992. Enthralled with modernity: The historical context of knowledge and theory development in public administration. *Public Administration Review* 52 (4): 363–73.

———. 2000. Uncovering the political philosophy of the new public management. *Administrative Theory & Praxis* 22 (3): 498–99.

Adams, Guy B., and Danny L. Balfour. 2004. *Unmasking administrative evil,* rev. ed. Armonk, NY: M. E. Sharpe.

———. 2009. *Unmasking administrative evil,* 3rd ed. Armonk, NY: M. E. Sharpe.

Adams, Guy B., and Jay D. White. 1994. Dissertation research in public administration and cognate fields: An assessment of methods and quality. *Public Administration Review* 54 (6): 565–76.

Adomavicius, Gediminas, Jesse C. Bockstedt, Alok Gupta, and Robert J. Kauffman. 2008. Making sense of technology trends in the information technology landscape: A design science approach. *MIS Quarterly* 32 (4): 779–809.

Agranoff, Robert. 1990. Managing federalism through human services intergovernmental bodies. *Publius* 20 (1): 1–22.

———. 2001. Managing within the matrix: Does collaborative federalism exist? *Publius* 31 (Summer): 31–56.

———. 2003. *Leveraging networks: A guide for public managers working across organizations.* Arlington, VA: IBM Endowment for the Business of Government.

———. 2007. *Managing within networks: Adding value to public organizations.* Washington, DC: Georgetown University Press.

Agranoff, Robert, and Michael McGuire. 1998. Multinetwork management: Collaboration and the hollow state in local economic policy. *Journal of Public Administration Research and Theory* 8 (1): 67–91.

———. 2001a. American federalism and the search for models of management. *Public Administration Review* 61 (6): 671–81.

———. 2001b. Big questions in public network management research. *Journal of Public Administration Research and Theory* 11 (3): 295–326.

———. 2003. *Collaborative public management: New strategies for local governments.* Washington, DC: Georgetown University Press.

REFERENCES

Agranoff, Robert, and Beryl A. Radin. 1991. The comparative case study approach in public administration. *Research in Public Administration* 1:203–31.

Allison, Graham T. 1979. Public and private management: Are they fundamentally alike in all unimportant respects? In *Proceedings for Public Management Research Conference*, 27–38. Washington, DC: Office of Personnel Management.

Amaratunga, Dilanthi, and David Baldry. 2001. Case study methodology as a means of theory building: Performance measurement in facilities management organisations. *Work Study* 50 (3): 95–105.

American Heritage guide to contemporary usage and style. 2005. Boston: Houghton Mifflin.

Anderson, Stephen H., and Natalia V. Smirnova. 2006. A study of executive budget-balancing decisions. *American Review of Public Administration* 36 (3): 323–36.

Andrews, Rhys. 2008. Perceived environmental uncertainty in public organizations: An empirical exploration. *Public Performance & Management Review* 32 (1): 25–50.

Andrews, Rhys, George A. Boyne, and Richard M. Walker. 2006. Strategy content and organizational performance: An empirical analysis. *Public Administration Review* 66 (1): 52–63.

Argyris, Chris. 1973a. Organization man: Rational and self-actualizing. *Public Administration Review* 33 (4): 354–57.

———. 1973b. Some limits of rational man organization theory. *Public Administration Review* 33 (3): 253–67.

Arsneault, Shelly. 2006. Implementing welfare reform in rural and urban communities: Why place matters. *American Review of Public Administration* 36 (2): 173–88.

Ash Center for Democratic Governance and Innovation. 2009. About us. John F. Kennedy School of Government, Harvard University. www.innovations.harvard.edu/about-us.html.

Aucoin, Peter. 1995. *The new public management: Canada in comparative perspective.* Montreal: McGill–Queen's University Press.

Auer, Matthew. 2007. The policy sciences in critical perspective. In *Handbook of public administration*, 3rd edition, ed. Jack Rabin, H. Bartley Hildreth, and Gerald J Miller, 541–62. New York: Taylor & Francis.

Babbie, Earl R. 2006. *The practice of social research*, 11th ed. Belmont, CA: Wadsworth.

Ban, Carolyn. 1995. *How do public managers manage? Bureaucratic constraints, organizational culture, and the potential for reform.* San Francisco: Jossey-Bass.

Bardach, Eugene. 1994. Comment: The problem of "best practice" research. *Journal of Policy Analysis and Management* 13 (2): 260–68.

Barzelay, Michael. 1992. *Breaking through bureaucracy: A new vision for managing in government.* Berkeley: University of California Press.

———. 2001. *The new public management.* Berkeley: University of California Press.

Behn, Robert D. 1988. Management by groping along. *Journal of Policy Analysis & Management* 8 (3): 643–63.

————. 1991. *Leadership counts: Lessons for public managers from the Massachusetts Welfare, Training, and Employment Program.* Cambridge, MA: Harvard University Press.

————. 1995. The big questions of public management. *Public Administration Review* 55 (4): 313–24.

————. 1996. Public management: Should it strive to be art, science, or engineering? *Journal of Public Administration Research and Theory* 6 (1): 91–123.

Bertelli, Anthony M., and Laurence E. Lynn Jr. 2006. *Madison's managers: Public administration and the Constitution.* Baltimore: Johns Hopkins University Press.

Binder, Carl. 1996. Behavioral fluency: Evolution of a new paradigm. *Behavior Analyst* 19 (2): 163–97.

Borins, Sandford. 1999. Trends in training public managers: A report on a commonwealth seminar. *International Public Management Journal* 2 (2): 299–314.

Borkovec, T. G., and L. G. Castonguay. 1998. What is the scientific meaning of "empirically supported therapy"? *Journal of Consulting and Clinical Psychology* 66 (1): 136–42.

Bouckaert, Geert. 2008. The administrative and academic politics of ranking research: The case of the 2004 "public sector performance" study in the Netherlands. *International Public Management Journal* 11 (3): 367–84.

Bowman, Ann O'M. 2004. Horizontal federalism: Exploring interstate interactions. *Journal of Public Administration Research and Theory* 14 (4): 535–46.

Bowman, James S. 2008. The research problem, method and serendipity: An investigator's journey. In *Handbook of research methods in public administration,* 2nd edition, ed. Kaifeng Yang and Gerald J. Miller, 93–108. New York: Taylor & Francis.

Box, Richard C. 1992. An examination of the debate over research in public administration. *Public Administration Review* 52 (1): 62–69.

————. 2005. Dialogue and *Administrative Theory & Praxis*: Twenty-five years of public administration theory. *Administrative Theory & Praxis* 27 (3): 438–66.

————, ed. 2007. *Democracy and public administration.* Armonk, NY: M. E. Sharpe.

Boyd, Christina L., Lee Epstein, and Henry Wade Rogers. Untangling the causal effects of sex on judging. Unpublished manuscript. http://epstein.law.northwestern.edu/research/genderjudging.pdf.

Boyne, George A. Julian S. Gould-Williams, Jennifer Law, and Richard M. Walker. 2004. Toward the self-evaluating organization? An empirical test of the Wildavsky model. *Public Administration Review* 64 (4): 463–73.

Bozeman, Barry, ed. 1993. *Public management: The state of the art.* San Francisco: Jossey-Bass.

————. 1987. *All organizations are public.* San Francisco: Jossey-Bass.

————. 2007. *Public value and public interest: Counterbalancing economic individualism.* Washington, DC: Georgetown University Press.

Bozeman, Barry, and Sanjay K. Pandey. 2004. Public management decision making: Effects of decision content. *Public Administration Review* 64 (5): 553–65.

Bradbury, Mark D. 2008. *Parents involved in Community Schools v. Seattle School, District No. 1*: Dubious prospects for diversity as a compelling governmental interest. *Review of Public Personnel Administration* 28 (4): 385–91.

Brady, Henry. and David Collier, eds. 2004. *Rethinking social inquiry: Diverse tools, shared standards.* Lanham, MD: Rowman & Littlefield.

Bray, Dennis, and Hans von Storch. 1999. Climate science: An empirical example of postnormal science. *Bulletin of the American Meteorological Society* 80 (3): 439–55.

Bremer, Kamala, and Deborah A. Howe. 1988. Strategies used to advance women's careers in the public service: Examples from Oregon. *Public Administration Review* 48 (6): 957–61.

Bretschneider, Stuart. 1990. Management information systems in public and private organizations: An empirical test. *Public Administration Review* 50 (5): 536–45.

Brewer, Gene A., Sally Coleman Selden, and Rex L. Facer II. 2000. Individual conceptions of public service motivation. *Public Administration Review* 60 (3): 254–64.

Brower, Ralph S., and Mitchel Y. Abolafia. 1997. Bureaucratic politics: The view from below. *Journal of Public Administration Research & Theory* 7 (2): 305–31.

Brower, Ralph S., Mitchel Y. Abolafia, and Jered B. Carr. 2000. On improving qualitative methods in public administration research. *Administration & Society* 32 (4): 363–97.

Brown, Steven. 1980. *Political subjectivity: Applications of q-methodology in political science.* New Haven, CT: Yale University Press.

Brudney, Jeffrey L. 1990. Expanding the government-by-proxy construct: Volunteers in the delivery of public services. *Nonprofit and Voluntary Sector Quarterly* 19 (4): 315–28.

Brudney, Jeffrey L., Laurence J. O'Toole, Jr. and Hal G. Rainey, eds. 2000. *Advancing public management: New developments in theory, methods, and practice.* Washington, DC: Georgetown University Press.

Bryson, John M., Barbara C. Crosby, and Melissa Middleton Stone. 2006. The design and implementation of cross-sector collaborations: Propositions from the literature. *Public Administration Review*, December (Special Issue), 44–55.

Bunge, Mario. 1983. Epistemology and methodology I: Exploring the world. *Treatise on basic philosophy*, vol. 5. Dordrecht: D. Reidel.

Burnier, DeLysa. 2006. Lost and found: Gender, narrative, Miss Burchfield, and the construction of knowledge in public administration. *Administrative Theory & Praxis* 28 (3): 444–64.

Burrell, Gibson, and Gareth Morgan. 1979. *Sociological paradigms and organizational analysis.* London: Heinemann.

Business Week. 1986. Special report: The hollow corporation. March 3, 56–85.

Callahan, Kathe, Melvin J. Dubnick, and Dorothy Olshfski. 2006. War narratives: Framing our understanding of the war on terror. *Public Administration Review* 66 (4): 554–68.

REFERENCES

Carnap, Rudolf. 1996. The elimination of metaphysics through logical analysis of language. In *Logical empiricism at its peak: Schlick, Carnap, and Neurath*, ed. Sahotra Sarkar, 10–32. New York: Garland.

Carroll, James D. 1987. Public administration in the third century of the Constitution: Supply-side management, privatization, or pubic investment? *Public Administration Review* 47 (1): 106–14.

Caruson, Kiki, and Susan A. MacManus. 2008. Disaster vulnerabilities: How strong a push toward regionalism and intergovernmental cooperation? *American Review of Public Administration* 38 (3): 286–306.

Cayer, N. Joseph, and Lee Sigelman. 1980. Minorities and women in state and local government: 1973–1975. *Public Administration Review* 40 (5): 443–50.

Chambless, D. L., and S. D. Hollon. 1998. Defining empirically supported therapies. *Journal of Consulting and Clinical Psychology* 66 (1): 7–18.

Charlesworth, James C., ed. 1968. *Theory and practice of public administration: Scope, objectives, and methods.* Philadelphia: American Academy of Political and Social Science.

Cheung, Anthony B. L. 2005. The politics of administrative reforms in Asia: Paradigms and legacies, paths and diversities. *Governance: An International Journal of Policy, Administration, and Institutions* 18 (2): 257–82.

Chih-Wei, Hsieh, and Elizabeth Winslow. 2006. Gender representation in the federal workforce. *Review of Public Personnel Administration* 26 (3): 276–94.

Christensen, Tom, and Per Laegreid. 2007. Introduction: Theoretical approach and research questions. In *Transcending new public management*, ed. Tom Christensen and Per Laegreid, 1–16. Hampshire, U.K.: Ashgate.

Cho, Chung-Lae. 2004. The devolution revolution in intergovernmental relations in the 1990s: Changes in cooperative and coercive state–national relations as perceived by state administrators. *Journal of Public Administration Research and Theory* 14 (4): 447–68.

Cigler, Beverly A. 1994. The county–state connection: A national study of associations of counties. *Public Administration Review* 54 (1): 3–11.

Clark, Vicki L. Plano, and John W. Creswell, eds. 2008. *The mixed methods reader.* Thousand Oaks, CA: Sage.

Cohen, Patricia. 2009. Field study: Just how relevant is political science? *New York Times*, October 20. pp. C1, C7.

Collins, R. 1986. Is 1980s sociology in the doldrums? *American Journal of Sociology* 91 (6): 1336–55.

Connell, Raewyn. 2006. Glass ceilings or gendered institutions? Mapping the gender regimes of public sector worksites. *Public Administration Review* 66 (6): 837–49.

Cooper, Phillip J. 1988. *Hard judicial choices: Federal district court judges and state and local officials.* New York: Oxford University Press.

———. 1999. *Battles on the bench: Conflict inside the Supreme Court.* Lawrence: University Press of Kansas.

———. 2002a. *By order of the president: The use and abuse of executive direct action.* Lawrence: University Press of Kansas.

———. 2002b. *Governing by contract: Challenges and opportunities for public managers.* Washington, DC: CQ Press.

Cooper, Terry L., and Thomas A. Bryer. 2007. William Robertson: Exemplar of politics and public management rightly understood. *Public Administration Review* 67 (5): 816–23.

Cooper, Terry L., and N. Dale Wright. 1992. *Exemplary public administrators: Character and leadership in government.* San Francisco: Jossey-Bass.

Crane, Diana, and Henry Small. 1992. American sociology since the seventies: The emerging identity crisis in the discipline. In *Sociology and its politics: The forms and fates of disciplinary organization,* ed. Terence Charles Halliday and Morris Janowitz, 197–234. Chicago: University of Chicago Press.

Creswell, John W. 2006. *Qualitative inquiry and research design: Choosing among five approaches,* 2nd ed. Thousand Oaks, CA: Sage.

———. 2009. *Research design: Qualitative, quantitative, and mixed methods approaches,* 3rd ed. Thousand Oaks, CA: Sage Publications.

Crotty, Michael. 1998. *The foundations of social research: Meaning and perspective in the research process.* Thousand Oaks, CA: Sage.

Cunningham, Robert, and Dorothy Olshfski. 1986. Interpreting state administrator–legislator relationships. *Western Political Science Quarterly* 39 (1): 104–17.

Dahl, Robert A. 1947. The science of public administration: Three problems. *Public Administration Review* 7 (1): 1–11.

Danziger, Marie. 1995. Policy analysis postmodernized. *Policy Studies Journal* 23 (3): 435–50.

deLeon, Peter. 1988. *Advice and consent: The development of the policy sciences.* New York: Russell Sage Foundation.

———. 1990. Participatory policy analysis: Prescriptions and precautions. *Asian Journal of Public Administration* 12 (2): 29–54.

———. 1997. *Democracy and the policy sciences.* Albany: State University of New York Press.

———. 1998. Models of policy discourse: Insights versus prediction. *Policy Studies Journal* 26 (1): 147–61.

Dempster, Beth. 1998. Toward a post-normal science: New (?) approaches to research. http://bethd.ca/webs/pnsresearch/index.html.

Denhardt, Janet Vinzant, and Robert B. Denhardt. 2001. Creating a culture of innovation: 10 lessons from America's best-run city. Arlington, VA: PricewaterhouseCoopers Endowment for the Business of Government.

———. 2007. *The new public service, expanded edition: Serving, not steering.* Armonk, NY: M. E. Sharpe.

Denhardt, Robert B. 1993. *The pursuit of significance: Strategies for managerial success in public organizations.* Belmont, CA: Wadsworth.

———. 2004. *Theories of public organization,* 4th ed. Belmont, CA: Wadsworth/ Thomson Learning.

Denzin, Norman K., and Yvonna S. Lincoln, eds. 2005. *The Sage handbook of qualitative research,* 3rd ed. Thousand Oaks, CA: Sage.

Dicke, Lisa A. 2002. Ensuring accountability in human services contracting. *American Review of Public Administration* 32 (4): 455–470.

DiIulio, John J. 1989. Recovering the public management variable: Lessons from schools, prisons, and armies. *Public Administration Review* 49 (2): 127–33.

Doig, Jameson W., and Erwin C. Hargrove, eds. 1987. *Leadership and innovation: A biographical perspective on entrepreneurs in government.* Baltimore: Johns Hopkins University Press.

Dolan, Julie. 2002. Representative bureaucracy in the federal executive: Gender and spending priorities. *Journal of Public Administration Research and Theory* 12 (3): 353–75.

Donmoyer, Robert. 2006. Take my paradigm . . . please! The legacy of Kuhn's construct in educational research. *International Journal of Qualitative Studies in Education* 19 (1): 11–34.

Drechsler, Wolfgang. 2005. The rise and demise of the new public management. www.paecon.net/PAEReview/issue33/Drechsler33.htm.

Dror, Yehezkel. 1967. Policy analysis: A new professional role in government service. *Public Administration Review* 27 (3): 197–203.

Drori, Israel, and Chaim Weizmann. 2007. Prime Minister Yitzhak Rabin against the settlers: A stakeholder analysis. *Public Administration Review* 67 (2): 302–14.

Drucker, Peter. 1952. "Development of theory of democratic administration": Replies and comments. *American Political Science Review* 46 (June): 496–500.

Dryzek, John S. 1990. *Discursive democracy: Politics, policy and political science.* Cambridge: Cambridge University Press.

Dubnick, Melvin J. 1999. Demons, spirits, and elephants: Reflections on the failure of public administration theory. Paper delivered at Annual Meeting of American Political Science Association, Atlanta, Georgia.

Duerst-Lahti, Georgia, and Rita Mae Kelly, eds. 1995. *Gender power, leadership and governance.* Ann Arbor: University of Michigan Press.

Dul, Jan, and Tony Hak. 2008. *Case study methodology in business research.* Burlington, MA: Butterworth-Heinemann/Elsevier.

Dunleavy, Patrick, Helen Margetts, Simon Bastow, and Jane Tinkler. 2006. New public management is dead—long live digital-era governance. *Journal of Public Administration Research and Theory* 16 (3): 467–94.

Durant, Robert F. 2007. Toxic politics, organization change, and the "greening" of the U.S. Military: Toward a polity-centered perspective. *Administration & Society* 39 (3): 409–46.

Durning, Dan. 1993. Participatory policy analysis in a social service agency: A case study. *Journal of Policy Analysis and Management* 12 (2): 297–322.

———. 1999. The transition from traditional to postpositivist policy analysis: A role for Q-methodology. *Journal of Policy Analysis and Management* 18 (3): 389–410.

Durning, Dan, and Will Osuna. 1994. Policy analysts' roles and orientation: An empirical investigation using q-methodology. *Journal of Policy Analysis and Management* 13 (4): 629–57.

Dye, Thomas. 1976. *Policy analysis*. Tuscaloosa: University of Alabama Press.

Elling Richard C., and T. Lyke Thompson. 2006. Human resource problems and state management performance across two decades: The implications for civil service reform. *Review of Public Personnel Administration* 26 (4): 302–34.

Ellwood, Charles A. 1930. The uses and limitations of behaviorism in sociology. *Papers of the American Sociological Society* 25: 74–82.

———. 1933. *Methods in sociology: A critical study*. Durham, NC: Duke University Press.

Ellwood, John W. 1996. Political science. In *The state of public management*, ed. Donald F. Kettl and H. Brinton Milward, 51–74. Baltimore: Johns Hopkins University Press.

Elman, Colin. 2008. Symposium on qualitative research methods in political science. *Journal of Politics* 70 (1): 272–74.

Emerson, Richard M. 1972. Exchange theory, part III: Exchange relations and networks. In *Sociological theories in progress*, ed. Joseph Berger, Morris Zelditch, and B. Anderson, 58–87. Boston: Houghton Mifflin.

Erickson, Frederick. 1986. Qualitative methods in research on teaching. In *Handbook of research on teaching*, 3rd edition, ed. Merlin C. Wittrock, 119–61. New York: Macmillan.

Eriksson, Darek M. 2006. Normative sources of systems thinking: An inquiry into religious ground-motives of systems thinking paradigms. In *In search of an integrative vision for technology*, ed. Sytse Strijbos and Andrew Basden, 217–34. New York: Springer.

Evans, Karen G., and Gary L. Wamsley. 1999. Where's the institution? Neoinstitutionalism and public management. In *Public management reform and innovation: Research, theory, and application*, ed. H. George Frederickson and Jocelyn Johnston, 117–44. Tuscaloosa: University of Alabama Press.

Fayol, Henri. 1916. Administration industrielle et générale. *Bulletin de la société de l'industrie minérale* (5th series) 10 (3): 5–162.

———. 1917. *Administration industrielle et générale*. Paris: Dunod et Pinat.

———. 1937. The administrative theory in the state. In *Papers on the Science of Administration*, ed. Luther Gulick and Lyndell Urwick, 99n114. New York: Institute of Public Administration.

Felts, Arthur A., and Philip H. Jos. 2000. Time and space: The origins and implications of the new public management. *Administrative Theory & Praxis* 22 (3): 519–33.

Ferber, Marianne A., and Julie A. Nelson, eds. 1993. *Beyond economic man: Feminist theory in economics*. Chicago: University of Chicago Press.

Ferguson, Kathy E. 1984. *The feminist case against bureaucracy*. Philadelphia: Temple University Press.

Fernandez, Sergio, and Craig R. Smith. 2005. Looking for evidence of public employee opposition to privatization: An empirical study with implications for practice. *Review of Public Personnel Administration* 26 (4): 356–81.

Fernández-Armesto, Felipe. 1997. *Truth: A history and a guide for the perplexed.* New York: St. Martin's Press.

Feyerabend, Paul. 1981. *Realism, rationalism, and scientific method.* New York: Cambridge University Press.

Finer, Herman. 1925. The civil service in the modern state. *American Political Science Review* 19 (2): 277–89.

Fischer, Frank. 1998. Beyond empiricism: Policy inquiry in postpositivist perspective. *Policy Studies Journal* 26 (1): 129–46.

———. 2000. *Citizens, experts, and the environment: The politics of local knowledge.* Durham, NC: Duke University Press.

———. 2003. *Reframing public policy: Discursive politics and deliberative practices.* New York: Oxford University Press.

Follett, Mary Parker. 1924. *Creative experience.* New York: Longman Green. (Reprinted 1951; New York: Peter Smith.)

Fountain, Jane E. 1994. Comment: Disciplining public management research. *Journal of Policy Analysis & Management* 13 (2): 269–77.

Fox, Charles J., and Hugh T. Miller. 1995. *Postmodern public administration: Toward discourse.* Thousand Oaks, CA: Sage.

Franco, Zeno, Harris Friedman, and Mike Arons. 2008. Are qualitative methods always best for humanistic psychology research? A conversation on the epistemological divide between humanistic and positive psychology. *Humanistic Psychologist* 36 (2): 159–203.

Franklin, Aimee L. 2001. Serving the public interest? Federal experiences with participation in strategic planning. *American Review of Public Administration* 31 (2): 126–38.

Frederickson, H. George. 1971. Toward a new public administration. In *Toward a new public administration: The Minnowbrook perspective,* ed. Frank Marini, 309–31. Scranton, PA: Chandler.

———. 1974. Social equity and public administration. *Public Administration Review* 34 (1): 1–2.

———. 1980. *New public administration.* Tuscaloosa: University of Alabama Press.

———. 1990. Public administration and social equity. *Public Administration Review* 50 (2): 228–37.

———. 1996. Comparing the reinventing government movement with the new public administration. *Public Administration Review* 56 (3): 263–70.

———. 1999. Introduction. In *Public management reform and innovation: Research, theory, and application,* ed. H. George Frederickson and Jocelyn Johnston, 1–10. Tuscaloosa: University of Alabama Press.

———. 2000. Can Bureaucracy Be Beautiful? *Public Administration Review* 60 (1): 47–53.

Frederickson, H. George, and Kevin B. Smith. 2003. *The public administration theory primer.* Boulder, CO: Westview Press.

Fuchs, Christian, and Marisol Sandoval. 2008. Positivism, postmodernism, or critical theory? A case study of communications students' understandings of criticism. *Journal for Critical Education Policy Studies* 6 (2): 12–141.

Funtowicz, Silvio O., and Jerome R. Ravetz. 1992. Three types of risk assessment and the emergence of post-normal science. In *Social theories of risk*, ed. S. Krimsky and D. Golding, 251–73. Westport, CT: Praeger.

———. 1993. Science for the post-normal age. *Futures* 25 (7): 739–55.

———. 1994. Emergent complex systems. *Futures* 26 (6): 568–82.

———. 2008. Post-normal science: Environmental policy under conditions of complexity. www.jvds.nl/pns/pns.htm.

Furlong, Scott R. 1998. Political influence on the bureaucracy: The bureaucracy speaks. *Journal of Public Administration Research and Theory* 8 (1): 39–65.

Gabrielian, Vache, Kaifeng Yang, and Susan Spice. 2008. Qualitative research methods. In *Handbook of research methods in public administration*, 2nd edition, ed. Kaifeng Yang and Gerald J. Miller, 141–68. New York: Taylor & Francis.

Gephart, Robert. 1999. Paradigms and research methods. *Academy of Management Research Methods Forum*, Summer. http://division.aomonline.org/rm/1999_RMD_Forum_Paradigms_and_Reseach_Methods.htm.

Gerring, John, and Craig W. Thomas. 2005. Comparability: A key issue in research design. www.concepts-methods.org/working_papers/20051012_42_PM%204%20 Gerring%20&%20Thomas.pdf.

Goertz, Gary. 2006. *Social science concepts: A user's guide*. Princeton, NJ: Princeton University Press.

Golden, Marissa Martino. 1998. Interest groups in the rule-making process: Who participates? Whose voices get heard? *Journal of Public Administration Research and Theory* 8 (2): 245–70.

Goodsell, Charles T. 2004. *The case for bureaucracy: A public administration polemic*, 4th ed. Washington, DC: CQ Press.

Gormley, William T., Jr. 1996. Regulatory privatization: A case study. *Journal of Public Administration Research & Theory* 6 (2): 243–60.

Gow, James Iain, and Caroline Dufour. 2000. Is the new public administration a paradigm? Does it matter? *International Review of Administrative Sciences* 66 (4): 573–97.

Grabosky, Peter N., and David H. Rosenbloom. 1975. Racial and ethnic integration in the federal service. *Social Science Quarterly* 56 (1): 71–84.

Greene, Jennifer C. 2007. *Mixed methods in social inquiry*. San Francisco: Jossey-Bass.

Guba, Egon G. 1990. *The paradigm dialog*. Newbury Park, CA: Sage Publications.

Gulick, Luther. 1937. Notes on the theory of organization. In *Papers on the science of administration*, ed. Luther Gulick and Lydell Urwick, 191–95. New York: Institute of Public Administration.

Gulick, Luther, and Lyndell Urwick, eds. 1937. *Papers on the science of administration*. New York: Institute of Public Administration.

Gunnell, John G. 1991. The historiography of American political science. In *The development of political science*, ed. David Easton, John G. Gunnell, and Luigi Graziano, 13–33. New York: Routledge.

Guy, Mary E., ed. 1992. *Women and men of the states: Public administrators at the state level.* Armonk, NY: M. E. Sharpe.

———. 1993. Three steps forward two steps backward: The status of women's integration into public management. *Public Administration Review* 53 (4): 285–92.

Guy, Mary E., and Meredith A. Newman. 2004. Women's jobs, men's jobs: Sex segregation and emotional labor. *Public Administration Review* 64 (3): 289–98.

Haight, David, and Clare Ginger. 2000. Trust and understanding in participatory policy analysis: The case of the Vermont Forest Resources Advisory Council. *Policy Studies Journal* 28 (4): 739–59.

Hale, Mary M., and Rita Mae Kelly. 1989. Gender, democracy, and representative bureaucracies. In *Gender, bureaucracy, and democracy*, ed. Mary M. Hale and Rita M. Kelly, 3–17. Westport, CT: Greenwood Press.

Hancock, Philip, and Melissa Tyler. 2001. *Work, postmodernism and organization: A critical introduction.* London: Sage.

Hardcastle, Gary. 2005. Logical empiricism. In *The philosophy of science: An encyclopedia*, vol. 1, ed. Sahotra Sarkar and Jessica Pfeifer, 458–65. New York: Routledge.

Harding, Sandra. 1987. Introduction: Is there a feminist method? In *Feminism and methodology: Social science issues*, ed. Sandra Harding, 1–14. Bloomington: Indiana University Press.

Harmon, Michael M. 1989. The Simon/Waldo debate: A review and update. *Public Administration Quarterly* 12 (4): 437–51.

Hawkesworth, Mary. 2006. Contending conceptions of science and politics: Methodology and the constitution of the political. In *Interpretation and method: Empirical research methods and the interpretive turn*, ed. Dvora Yanow and Peregrine Schwartz-Shea, 27–49. Armonk, NY: M. E. Sharpe.

Hays, Steven W., and Richard C. Kearney. 2001. Anticipated changes in human resource management: Views from the field. *Public Administration Review* 61 (5): 585–97.

Healy, Marilyn, and Chad Perry. 2000. Comprehensive criteria to judge validity and reliability of qualitative research within the realism paradigm. *Qualitative Market Research: An International Journal* 3 (3): 118–26.

Heinrich, Carolyn J. 1999. Do government bureaucrats make effective use of performance information? *Journal of Public Administration Research and Theory* 9 (3): 363–93.

Henderson, Lawrence Joseph. 1935. *Pareto's general sociology.* Cambridge, MA: Harvard University Press.

Henry, Nicholas. 2006. *Public administration and public affairs*, 10th ed. Upper Saddle River, NJ: Prentice Hall.

Herzog, Richard J. 1993. Building practitioner-held theory through triangulation. *Journal of Public Administration Research and Theory* 3 (4): 431–56.

Hildreth, W. Bartley. 2009. The financial logistics of disaster: The case of hurricane Katrina. *Public Performance & Management Review* 32 (3): 400–436.

Hildreth, W. Bartley, and Gerald J. Miller. 2002. Debt and the local economy: Problems in benchmarking local government debt affordability. *Public Budgeting & Finance* 22 (4): 99–113.

Hindera, John J. 1993. Representative bureaucracy: Imprimis evidence of active representation in the EEOC district offices. *Social Science Quarterly* 74 (1): 95–108.

Ho, Alfred. 2007. The governance challenges of the Government Performance and Results Act: A case study of the Substance Abuse and Mental Health Administration. *Public Performance & Management Review* 30 (3): 369–97.

Hodgkinson, Gerard P., and Mark P. Healey. 2008. Toward a (pragmatic) science of strategic intervention: Design propositions for scenario planning. *Organization Studies* 29 (3): 435–57.

Homans, George C. 1950. *The human group*. New York: Harcourt, Brace.

———. 1958. Social behavior as exchange. *American Journal of Sociology* 63 (6): 507–606.

Hood, Christopher. 1991. A public management for all seasons? *Public Administration* 69 (1): 3–19.

———. 2007. Public Management: The word, the movement, the science. In *The Oxford handbook of public management*, ed. Ewan Ferlie, Laurence E. Lynn Jr., and Christopher Pollitt, 7–26. Oxford: Oxford University Press.

Horiuchi, Catherine. 2005. The rational feminist: Enhancing administration theory through objective models. *Administrative Theory & Praxis* 27 (2): 377–84.

Houston, David J., and Sybil M. Delevan. 1990. Public administration research: An assessment of journal publications. *Public Administration Review* 50 (6): 674–81.

Howell-Moroney, Michael. 2008. A mixed method look at state growth management policy. *American Review of Public Administration* 38 (3): 339–61.

Huang, Kun, and Keith G. Provan. 2007. Resource tangibility and patterns of interaction in a publicly funded health and human services network. *Journal of Public Administration Research and Theory* 17 (3): 435–54.

Hummel, Ralph P. 1991. Stories managers tell: Why they are as valid as science. *Public Administration Review* 51 (1): 31–41.

———. 1996. Post-modernism and a reasonable philosophy. *Administrative Theory & Praxis* 18 (1): 45–47.

———. 2006. "We don't need no stinking badges"—Modernists vs. post-modernists: Kant, Foucault, Weber, Loewith, Arendt. *Administrative Theory & Praxis* 28 (3): 311–29.

———. 2007. *The bureaucratic experience: The post-modern challenge*, 5th ed. Armonk, NY: M. E. Sharpe.

Hutchinson, Janet R. 2005. Forum: PA feminisms, with a note on gender anarchy. *Administrative Theory & Praxis* 27 (2): 358–63.

REFERENCES

Hutchinson, Janet R., and Deirdre M. Condit. 2009. Being there matters—redefining the model public servant: Viola O. Baskerville in profile. *Public Administration Review* 69 (1): 29–38.

Hutchinson, Janet R., and Hollie S. Mann. 2004. Feminist praxis: Administering for a multicultural, multigendered culture. *Administrative Theory and Praxis* 26 (1): 79–95.

————. 2006. Gender anarchy and the future of feminism in public administration. *Administrative Theory and Praxis* 28 (3): 399–417.

Ingraham, Patricia W. 1995. *The foundation of merit public service in American democracy.* Baltimore: Johns Hopkins University Press.

————, ed. 2007. *In pursuit of performance: Management systems in state and local government.* Baltimore: Johns Hopkins University Press.

Ingraham, Patricia W., and Barbara S. Romzek. 1994. *New paradigms for government: Issues for the changing public service.* San Francisco: Jossey-Bass.

Jang, Hee Soun, and Richard C. Feiock. 2007. Public versus private funding of nonprofit organizations: Implications for collaboration. *Public Performance & Management Review* 31 (2): 174–90.

Jensen, Jason L., and Robert Rodgers. 2001. Cumulating the intellectual gold of case study research. *Public Administration Review* 61 (2): 235–46.

Kaboolian, Linda. 1996. Sociology. In *The state of public management,* ed. Donald F. Kettl and H. Brinton Milward, 75–91. Baltimore: Johns Hopkins University Press.

Kadushin, Charles, Shahar Hecht, Theodore Sasson, and Leonard Saxe. 2008. Triangulation and mixed methods designs: Practicing what we preach in the evaluation of an Israel experience educational program. *Field Methods* 20 (1): 46–65.

Kaplan, Thomas J. 1986. The narrative structure of policy analysis. *Journal of Policy Analysis & Management* 5 (4): 761–78.

Kaufman, Herbert. 1956. Emerging conflicts in the doctrines of public administration. *American Political Science Review* 50 (December): 1057–73.

————. 1960. *The forest ranger: A study in administrative behavior.* Baltimore: Johns Hopkins University Press.

Keiser, Lael R., Vicky M. Wilkins, Kenneth J. Meier, and Catherine Holland. 2002. Lipstick and logarithms: Gender, institutional context, and representative bureaucracy. *American Political Science Review* 96 (3): 553–64.

Kelle, Udo, and Heather Laurie. 1995. Computer use in qualitative research and issues of validity. In *Computer-aided qualitative data analysis: Theory, methods and practice,* ed. U. Kelle, 19–28. London: Sage.

Kellough, J. Edward. 1990. Integration in the public workplace: Determinants of minority and female employment in federal agencies. *Public Administration Review* 50 (5): 557–66.

————. 2006. *Understanding affirmative action: Politics, discrimination, and the search for justice.* Washington, DC: Georgetown University Press.

Kellough, J. Edward, and Lloyd G. Nigro. 2002. Pay for performance in Georgia state government: Employee perspectives on GeorgiaGain after 5 years. *Review of Public Personnel Administration* 22 (2): 146–66.

Kenworthy, Lane. 2008. Symposium on qualitative research methods in political science, book review: *Necessary conditions: Theory, methodology, and applications*, edited by Gary Goertz and Harvey Starr (Rowman and Littlefield, 2003). *Journal of Politics* 70 (1): 278–79.

Kettl, Donald F. 1993. Searching for clues about public management: Slicing the onion different ways. In *Public management: The state of the art*, ed. Barry Bozeman, 55–68. San Francisco: Jossey-Bass.

———. 2005. *The global public management revolution*, 2nd ed. Washington, DC: Brookings Institution Press.

Kettl, Donald F., and H. Brinton Milward, eds. 1996. *The state of public management*. Baltimore: Johns Hopkins University Press.

Kim, Soonhee. 2002. Participative management and job satisfaction: Lessons for management leadership. *Public Administration Review* 62 (2): 231–41.

Kim, Soonhee, and Hyangsoo Lee. 2006. The impact of organizational context and information technology on employee knowledge-sharing capabilities. *Public Administration Review* 66 (3): 370–85.

King, Cheryl Simrell, Kathryn M. Feltey, and Bridget O'Neill Susel. 2001. The question of participation: Toward authentic public participation in public administration. In *Bureaucracy, democracy and the study of administration*, ed. Camilla Stivers, 301–24. Boulder, CO: Westview Press.

King, Gary, Robert Keohane, and Sidney Verba. 1994. *Designing social inquiry: Scientific inference in qualitative research*. Princeton, NJ: Princeton University Press.

Kingsley, J. Donald. 1944. *Representative bureaucracy: An interpretation of the British civil service*. Yellow Springs, OH: Antioch Press.

Kitcher, Philip. 2001. *Science, truth, and democracy*. New York: Oxford University Press.

Kranz, Harry. 1976. *The participatory bureaucracy: Women and minorities in a more representative public service*. Lexington, MA: Lexington Books.

Krislov, Samuel. 1974. *Representative bureaucracy*. Englewood Cliffs, NJ: Prentice Hall.

Krislov, Samuel, and David H. Rosenbloom. 1981. *Representative bureaucracy and the American political system*. New York: Praeger.

Krueathep, Weerasak, Norma M. Riccucci, and Charas Suwanmala. 2010. Why do agencies work together? The determinants of network formation at the subnational level of government in Thailand. *Journal of Public Administration Research and Theory* 20 (1): 157–85.

Kuhlmann, Sabinem, Jörg Bogumil, and Stephan Grohs. 2008. Evaluating administrative modernization in German local governments: Success or failure of the "new steering model"? *Public Administration Review* 68 (5): 851–63.

REFERENCES

Kuhn, Thomas S. 1962. *The structure of scientific revolutions.* Chicago: University of Chicago Press.

———. 1996. *The structure of scientific revolutions,* 3rd ed. Chicago: University of Chicago Press.

Lakatos, Imre, and Alan Musgrave. 1970. *Criticism and growth of knowledge.* Cambridge: Cambridge University Press.

Lan, Zhiyong, and Kathleen K. Anders. 2000. A paradigmatic view of contemporary public administration research: An empirical test. *Administration & Society* 32 (2): 138–65.

Lasswell, Harold D. 1951. The policy orientation. In *The policy sciences,* ed. Daniel Lerner and Harold D. Lasswell, 3–15. Stanford, CA: Stanford University Press.

Lasswell, Harold D., and Myres S. McDougal. 1943. Legal education and public policy: Professional training in the public interest. *Yale Law Journal* 52 (2): 203–95.

Laugharne, Richard, and Jonathan Laugharne. 2002. Psychiatry, postmodernism and post-normal science. *Journal of Royal Society of Medicine* 95 (4): 207–10.

Law, David. 1993. *The rhetoric of empiricism: Language and perception from Locke to I. A. Richards.* Ithaca, NY: Cornell University Press.

Lee, Mordecai. 2003. The first federal public information service, 1920–1933: At the US Bureau of Efficiency. *Public Relations Review* 29 (4): 415–25.

———. 2006a. Empirical experiments in public reporting. *Public Administration Review* 66 (2): 252–62.

———. 2006b. *Institutionalizing Congress and the presidency: The U.S. Bureau of Efficiency, 1916–1933.* College Station: Texas A&M University Press.

Lejano, Raul. 2008. The phenomenon of collective action: Modeling institutions as structures of care. *Public Administration Review* 68 (3): 491–504.

Leplin, Jarrett. 1984. *Scientific realism.* Berkeley: University of California Press.

Light, Paul C. 2006. The tides of reform revisited: Patterns in making government work, 1945–2002. *Public Administration Review* 66 (1): 6–19.

Lin, Ann Chih. 1998. Bridging positivist and interpretivist approaches to qualitative methods. *Policy Studies Journal* 26 (1): 162–80.

Lincoln, Yvonna S., and Egon G. Guba. 1985. *Naturalistic inquiry.* Beverly Hills, CA: Sage.

———. 2000. Paradigmatic controversies, contradictions, and emerging confluences. In *Handbook of qualitative research,* 2nd edition, ed. Norman K. Denzin and Yvonna S. Lincoln, 163–88. Thousand Oaks, CA: Sage.

Lindblom, Charles E. 1990. *Inquiry and change.* New Haven, CT: Yale University Press.

Lipsey, Mark W. 1974. Psychology: Preparadigmatic, postparadigmatic, or misparadigmatic? *Science Studies* 4 (4): 406–10.

Lipsky, Michael. 1980. *Street-level bureaucracy: Dilemmas of the individual in public services.* New York: Russell Sage Foundation.

Little, John H. 2000. Between positivism and relativism: A middle path for pubic administration. Paper presented at Thirteenth Annual Conference of Public Administration Theory Network, Fort Lauderdale, January 28–29.

Long, Mark C. 2007. Affirmative action and its alternatives in public universities: What do we know? *Public Administration Review* 67 (2): 315–30.

Luton, Larry S. 2007a. Deconstructing public administration empiricism. *Administration & Society* 39 (4): 527–44.

———. 2007b. Digging deeply 47 years later: Herbert Kaufman's *The forest ranger. Public Administration Review* 67 (1): 165–68.

Lynn, Laurence E., Jr. 1994. Public management research: The triumph of art over science. *Journal of Policy Analysis and Management* 13 (2): 231–59.

———. 1996. *Public management as art, science, and profession.* Chatham, NJ: Chatham House.

———. 2001. The myth of the bureaucratic paradigm: What traditional public administration really stood for. *Public Administration Review* 61 (2): 144–60.

Lynn, Laurence E., Jr., Carolyn J. Heinrich, and Carolyn J. Hill. 2008. The empiricist goose has not been cooked! *Administration & Society* 40 (1): 104–9.

MacIver, R. M. 1930. Is sociology a natural science? *Papers of the American Sociological Society* 25: 25–35.

March, James M., and Herbert A. Simon. 1958. *Organizations.* New York: John Wiley & Sons.

March, Salvatore T., and Veda C. Storey. 2008. Design science in the information systems discipline: An introduction to the special issue on design science research. *MIS Quarterly* 32 (4): 725–30.

Marini, Frank, ed. 1971. *Toward a new public administration: The Minnowbrook perspective.* Scranton, PA: Chandler.

Mathiasen, David. 1999. The new public management and its critics. *International Public Management Journal* 2 (1): 90–111.

Mathieson, Kieran. 2007. Towards a design science of ethical decision support. *Journal of Business Ethics* 76 (3): 269–92.

Maxwell, Joseph. A. 2005. *Qualitative research design: An interactive approach*, 2nd ed. Thousand Oaks, CA: Sage.

May, Steve, and Dennis K. Mumby. 2005. Engaging organizational communication theory and research: Multiple perspectives. Thousand Oaks, CA: Sage.

Maynard-Moody, Steven, and Michael Musheno. 2003. *Cops, teachers, counselors: Stories from the front lines of public service.* Ann Arbor: University of Michigan Press.

———. 2006. Stories for research. In *Interpretation and method: Empirical research methods and the interpretive turn*, ed. Dvora Yanow and Peregrine Schwartz-Shea, 316–30. Armonk, NY: M. E. Sharpe.

Maynard-Moody, Steven, Donald D. Stull, and Jerry Mitchell. 1986. Reorganization as status drama: Building, maintaining and displacing dominant subcultures. *Public Administration Review* 46 (4): 301–10.

McCrary, Justin. 2007. The effect of court-ordered hiring quotas on the composition and quality of police. *American Economic Review* 97 (1): 318–53.

McCurdy, Howard E., and Robert E. Cleary. 1984. Why can't we resolve the research issue in public administration? *Public Administration Review* 44 (1): 49–56.

McGinn, Kathy, and Patricia M. Patterson. 2005. Along way toward what? Sex, gender, feminism, and the study of public administration. *International Journal of Public Administration* 28 (11–12): 929–42.

McGrath, Alister E. 2001. *Christian theology: An introduction*, 3rd ed. Malden, MA: Blackwell.

McNabb, David E. 2002. *Research methods in public administration and nonprofit management: Quantitative and qualitative approaches*. Armonk, NY: M. E. Sharpe.

———. 2004. *Research methods for political science: Quantitative and qualitative methods*. Armonk, NY: M. E. Sharpe.

———. 2008. *Research methods in public administration and nonprofit management: Quantitative and qualitative approaches*, 2nd ed. Armonk, NY: M. E. Sharpe.

McSwite, O. C. 1996. Postmodernism, public administration, and the public interest. In *Refounding democratic public administration: Modern paradoxes, postmodern challenges*, ed. Gary L. Wamsley and James F. Wolf, 198–224. Thousand Oaks, CA: Sage.

———. 1997. *Legitimacy in public administration: A discourse analysis*. Thousand Oaks, CA: Sage.

———. 2002. *An invitation to public administration*. Armonk, NY: M. E. Sharpe.

Medema, Steven G., and Warren J. Samuels, eds. 2003. *The history of economic thought: A reader*. New York: Routledge.

Meier, Kenneth J. 1975. Representative bureaucracy: An empirical analysis. *American Political Science Review* 69 (2): 526–42.

———. 1993a. Latinos and representative bureaucracy: Testing the Thompson and Henderson hypotheses. *Journal of Public Administration Research and Theory* 3 (4): 393–415.

———. 1993b. Representative bureaucracy: A theoretical and empirical exposition. In *Research in public administration*, ed. James Perry, 1–35. Greenwich, CT: JAI Press.

———. 2005. Public administration and the myth of the positivism: The antichrist's view. *Administrative Theory & Praxis* 27 (4): 650–68.

Meier, Kenneth J., and Lloyd G. Nigro. 1976. Representative bureaucracy and policy preferences: A study in the attitudes of federal executives. *Public Administration Review* 36 (4): 458–69.

Meier, Kenneth J., and Laurence J. O'Toole, Jr. 2001. Managerial strategies and behavior in networks: A model with evidence from U.S. public education. *Journal of Public Administration Research and Theory* 11 (3): 271–93.

———. 2002. Public management and organizational performance: The effect of managerial quality. *Journal of Policy Analysis and Management* 21 (4): 629–643.

————. 2003. Public management and educational performance: The impact of managerial networking. *Public Administration Review* 63 (6): 689–99.

Meier, Kenneth J., and Kevin B. Smith. 1994. Representative democracy and representative bureaucracy: Examining the top-down and bottom-up linkages. *Social Science Quarterly* 75 (4): 790–803.

Meier, Kenneth J., and Joseph Stewart Jr. 1992. Active representation in educational bureaucracies: Policy impacts. *American Review of Public Administration* 22: 157–71.

Meier, Kenneth J., Joseph Stewart Jr., and Robert E. England. 1989. *Race, class and education: The politics of second generation discrimination.* Madison: University of Wisconsin Press.

Meier, Kenneth J., Robert D. Wrinkle, and J. L. Polinard. 1999. Representative bureaucracy and distributional equity: Addressing the hard question. *Journal of Politics* 61 (4): 1025–39.

Melitski, James. 2003. Capacity and e-government performance: An analysis based on early adopters of Internet technologies in New Jersey. *Public Performance & Management Review* 26 (4): 376–90.

Metcalf, Henry Clayton, and Lyndell Fownes Urwick. 1942. *Dynamic administration: The collected papers of Mary Parker Follett.* New York: Harper & Brothers.

Miles, Matthew B., and A. Michael Huberman. 1994. *Qualitative data analysis: An expanded sourcebook*, 2nd ed. Thousand Oaks, CA: Sage.

Miller, Hugh T. 2002. *Postmodern public policy.* Albany: State University of New York Press.

————. 2008. Theory. In *Handbook of research methods in public administration*, 2nd edition, ed. Kaifeng Yang and Gerald J. Miller, 13–24. New York: Taylor & Francis.

Miller, Hugh T., and Charles J. Fox. 2006. *Postmodern public administration*, rev. ed. Armonk, NY: M. E. Sharpe.

Milward, H. Brinton. 1994. Nonprofit contracting and the hollow state. *Public Administration Review* 54 (1) 73–77.

————. 1996. Symposium on the hollow state: Capacity, control and performance in intergovernmental settings. *Journal of Public Administration Research and Theory* 6 (2): 193–95.

Milward, H. Brinton, and Keith G. Provan. 1993. The hollow state: Private provision of public services. In *Public Policy and Democracy*, ed. Helen Ingram and Steven Rathgeb Smith, 222–37. Washington, DC: Brookings Institution Press.

————. 2000. Governing the hollow state. *Journal of Public Administration Research and Theory* 10 (2): 359–79.

Milward, H. Brinton, Keith G. Provan, and Barbara A. Else. 1993. What does the hollow state look like? In *Public management: The state of the art*, ed. Barry Bozeman, 309–22. San Francisco: Jossey-Bass.

Moe, Terry M. 1984. The new economics of organization. *American Journal of Political Science* 28 (4): 38.

Moon, M. Jae, and Stuart Bretschneider. 2002. Does the perception of red tape constrain IT innovativeness in organizations? Unexpected results from a simultaneous equation model and implications. *Journal of Public Administration Research and Theory* 12 (2): 273–91.

Mosher, Frederick C. 1968. *Democracy and the public service.* New York: Oxford University Press.

———, ed. 1975. *American public administration: Past, present, future.* Tuscaloosa: University of Alabama Press.

Moynihan, Donald P. 2006. Managing for results in state government: Evaluating a decade of reform. *Public Administration Review* 66 (1): 77–89.

———. 2009. "Our usable past": A historical contextual approach to administrative values. *Public Administration Review* 69 (5): 813–22.

Moynihan, Donald P., and Sanjay K. Pandey. 2007. The role of organizations in fostering public service motivation. *Public Administration Review* 67 (1): 40–53.

Muller, Adrian. 2003. A flower in full blossom? Ecological economics at the crossroads between normal and postnormal science. *Ecological Economics* 45 (1): 19–27.

Myers, Jason. 2002. The truth about false consciousness. *Contemporary Political Theory* 1 (2): 139–56.

Nachmias, David, and David H. Rosenbloom. 1973. Measuring bureaucratic representation and integration. *Public Administration Review* 33 (6): 590–97.

Naff, Katherine C. 1994. Through the glass ceiling: Prospects for the advancement of women in the federal civil service. *Public Administration Review* 54 (6): 507–14.

———. 2001. *To look like America: Dismantling barriers for women and minorities in government.* Boulder, CO: Westview Press.

Naff, Katherine C., and John Crum. 2000. The president and representative bureaucracy: Rhetoric and reality. *Public Administration Review* 60 (2): 98–110.

Nalbandian, John. 1989. The U.S. Supreme Court's "consensus" on affirmative action. *Public Administration Review* 49 (1): 38–45.

Naylor, Lorenda A., and David H. Rosenbloom. 2004. *Adarand, Grutter,* and *Gratz*: Does affirmative action in federal employment matter? *Review of Public Personnel Administration* 24 (2): 150–74.

Newcomer, Kathryn E. 2007. How does program performance assessment affect program management in the federal government? *Public Performance & Management Review* 30 (3): 332–50.

Niiniluoto, Ilkka. 1999. *Critical scientific realism.* New York: Oxford University Press.

Nolan, Lawrence. 2005. The role of the imagination in rationalist philosophies of mathematics. In *A companion to rationalism,* ed. Alan Nelson, 224–49. Oxford: Blackwell.

Oberschall, Anthony. 1972. The institutionalization of American sociology. In *The establishment of empirical sociology: Studies in continuity, discontinuity, and institutionalization,* ed. Anthony Oberschall, 187–251. New York: Harper & Row.

O'Leary, Rosemary. 1995. *Environmental change: Federal courts and the EPA*. Philadelphia: Temple University Press.

———. 2006. *The ethics of dissent: Managing guerrilla government*. Washington, DC: CQ Press.

O'Leary, Rosemary, and Lisa Blomgren Bingham, eds. 2009. *The collaborative public manager: New ideas for the twenty-first century*. Washington, DC: Georgetown University Press.

O'Leary, Rosemary, and Susan Summers Raines. 2001. Lessons learned from two decades of alternative dispute resolution programs and processes at the U.S. Environmental Protection Agency. *Public Administration Review* 61 (6): 682–92.

Osborne, David, and Ted Gaebler. 1992. *Reinventing government*. Reading, MA: Addison-Wesley.

Ospina, Sonia M., and Jennifer Dodge. 2005. It's about time: Catching method up to meaning—the usefulness of narrative inquiry in public administration research. *Public Administration Review* 65 (2): 143–57.

Ostrom, Vincent. 2008. *The intellectual crisis in American public administration*, 3rd ed. Tuscaloosa: University of Alabama Press.

O'Toole, Laurence J., Jr., and Kenneth J. Meier. 2004a. Desperately seeking Selznick: Cooptation and the dark side of public management in networks. *Public Administration Review* 64 (6): 681–93.

———. 2004b. Public management in intergovernmental networks: Matching structural networks and managerial networking. *Journal of Public Administration Research and Theory* 14 (4): 469–94.

Ott, J. Steven, Albert C. Hyde, and Jay M. Shafritz, eds. 1991. *Public management: The essential readings*. Chicago: Nelson-Hall.

Page, Stephen. 2005. What's new about the New Public Management? Administrative change in the human services. *Public Administration Review* 65 (6): 713–27.

Patton, Michael Quinn. 1990. *Qualitative evaluation and research methods*. Newbury Park, CA: Sage.

———. 2001. *Qualitative research and evaluation methods*, 3rd ed. Thousand Oaks, CA: Sage.

Percival, Garrick L. 2009. Exploring the influence of local policy networks on the implementation of drug policy reform: The case of California's Substance Abuse and Crime Prevention Act. *Journal of Public Administration Research and Theory* 19 (4): 795–815.

Perry, James L. 1991. Strategies for building public administration theory. In *Research in public administration*, ed. James L. Perry, 1–18. Greenwich, CT: JAI Press.

———. 1993. Public Management theory: What is it? What should it be? In *Public management: The state of the art*, ed. Barry Bozeman, 16–18. San Francisco: Jossey-Bass.

———. 1996. *Handbook of public administration*, 2nd ed. San Francisco: Jossey-Bass.

REFERENCES

Perry, James L., and Kenneth L. Kraemer. 1986. Research methodology in the *Public Administration Review*, 1975–1984. *Public Administration Review* 46 (3): 215–26.

———. 1990. Research methodology in the public administration: Issues and patterns. In *Public administration: The state of the discipline*, ed. Naomi Lynn and Aaron Wildavsky, 347–72. Chatham, NJ: Chatham House.

Pielke, Roger A., Jr. 2004. What future for the policy sciences? *Policy Sciences* 37 (3–4): 209–25.

Poincaré, Jules Henri. *La Science et l'Hypothèse (Science and Hypothesis)*. Paris: Flammarion.

Poister, Theodore H., and John Clayton Thomas. 2007. The wisdom of crowds: Learning from administrators' perceptions of citizen perceptions. *Public Administration Review* 67 (2): 279–89.

Pollitt, Christopher, and Geert Bouckaert. 2004. *Public management reform: A comparative perspective*, 2nd ed. Oxford: Oxford University Press.

Popper, Karl. 1963. *Conjectures and refutations: The growth of scientific knowledge*. London: Routledge.

———. 1977. *The logic of scientific discovery*. London: Routledge.

Prottas Jeffrey M. 1979. *People processing: The street-level bureaucrat in public service bureaucracies*. Lexington, MA: Lexington Books.

Provan, Keith G., Kun Huang, and H. Brinton Milward. 2009. The evolution of structural embeddedness and organizational social outcomes in a centrally governed health and human services network. *Journal of Public Administration Research and Theory* 19 (4): 873–93.

Pynes, Joan E. 2000. Are women underrepresented as leaders of nonprofit organizations? *Review of Public Personnel Administration* 20 (2): 35–49.

Quade, Edward S. 1975. *Analysis for public decisions*. New York: Elsevier.

Raadschelders, Joseph C. N. 1999. A coherent framework for the study of public administration. *Journal of Public Administration Research and Theory* 9 (2): 281–303.

———. 2005. Symposium: Approaches to the study of public administration: Unified knowledge—competing approaches—methodological pluralism. *Administrative Theory & Praxis* 27 (4): 595–601.

Radin, Beryl A. 1997. The evolution of the policy analysis field: From conversation to conversations. *Journal of Policy Analysis and Management* 16 (2): 204–18.

———. 2000. *Beyond Machiavelli: Policy analysis comes of age*. Washington, DC: Georgetown University Press.

———. 2006. *Challenging the performance movement: Accountability, complexity and democratic values*. Washington, DC: Georgetown University Press.

———. 2007. Qualified to learn the job: Donna Shalala. *Public Administration Review* 67 (3): 504–10.

Rainey, Hal. G. 1990. Public management: Recent developments and current prospects. In *Public administration: State of the discipline*, ed. Naomi Lynn and Aaron Wildavsky, 157–84. Chatham, NJ: Chatham House.

————. 1994. On paradigms, progress, and prospects for public management. *Journal of Public Administration Research and Theory* 94 (1): 41–48.

————. 2003. *Understanding and managing public organizations*, 3rd ed. San Francisco: Jossey-Bass.

Rainey, Hal G., and James Thompson. 2006. Leadership and the transformation of a major institution: Charles Rossotti and the Internal Revenue Service. *Public Administration Review* 66 (4): 596–604.

Ravetz, Jerome R. 1999. What is post-normal science? *Futures* 31 (7): 647–53.

————. 2002. Food safety, quality, and ethics: A post-normal perspective. *Journal of Agricultural and Environmental Ethics* 15 (3): 255–65.

Reed, Mike. 1993. Organizations and modernity: Continuity and discontinuity in organization theory. In *Postmodernism and organizations*, ed. John Hassard and Martin Parker, 163–82. London: Sage.

Reichardt, Charles S., and Sharon F. Rallis, eds. 1994. *The qualitative–quantitative debate: New perspectives*. San Francisco: Jossey-Bass.

Rhodes, R. A. W. 2005. Everyday life in a ministry: Public administration as anthropology. *American Review of Public Administration* 35 (1): 3–25.

Ricci, David M. 1984. *The tragedy of political science: Politics, scholarship, and democracy*. New Haven, CT: Yale University Press.

Riccucci, Norma M. 1995. *Unsung heroes: Federal execucrats making a difference*. Washington, DC: Georgetown University Press.

————. 2001. The "old" public management vs. the "new" public management: Where does public administration fit in? *Public Administration Review* 61 (2): 172–75.

————. 2005. *How management matters: Street-level bureaucrats and welfare reform*. Washington, DC: Georgetown University Press.

————. 2006. The criteria of action in reforming and advancing the administrative state: How do we determine or 'know' effectiveness? In *Revisiting Dwight Waldo's administrative state*, ed. David H. Rosenbloom and Howard E. McCurdy, 55–70. Washington, DC: Georgetown University Press.

————. 2007a. The ethical responsibilities of street-level bureaucrats under welfare reform. *Public Integrity* 9 (2): 155–73.

————. 2007b. Moving away from a strict scrutiny standard for affirmative action: Implications for public management. *American Review of Public Administration* 37 (2): 123–41.

Riccucci, Norma M., and Marcia Meyers. 2004. Linking passive and active representation: The case of front-line workers in welfare agencies. *Journal of Public Administration Research and Theory* 14 (4): 585–97.

Riccucci, Norma M., Marcia Meyers, Irene Lurie, and Jun Seop Han. 2004. The implementation of welfare reform policy: The role of public managers in front-line practices. *Public Administration Review* 64 (4): 438–48.

Rice, Mitchell F., and Maurice Mongkuo. 1998. Did *Adarand* kill minority set-asides? *Public Administration Review* 58 (1): 82–86.

Richardson, George P. 1991. *Feedback thought in social science and systems theory.* Philadelphia: University of Pennsylvania Press.

Ritchie, Jane, and Jane Lewis, eds. 2003. *Qualitative research practice: A guide for social science students and researchers.* Thousand Oaks, CA: Sage.

Roberts, Alasdair. 2004. A partial revolution: The diplomatic ethos and transparency in intergovernmental organizations. *Public Administration Review* 64 (4): 410–24.

Roberts, Nancy C., and Raymond Trevor Bradley 1999. Research methodology for new public management. www.inpuma.net/research/papers/siena/roberts.doc.

Roberts, Robert N. 1988. *White house ethics: A history of the politics of conflict of interest regulation.* Westport, CT: Greenwood Press.

———. 2007. Developments in the law: *Garcetti v. Ceballos* and the workplace freedom of speech rights of public employees. *Public Administration Review* 67 (4): 662–72.

Robinson, Scott E., and Kenneth J. Meier. 2006. Path dependence and organizational behavior: Bureaucracy and social promotion. *American Review of Public Administration* 36 (3): 241–60.

Rockloff, Susan F., and Susan A. Moore. 2006. Assessing representation at different scales of decision making: Rethinking local is better. *Policy Studies Journal* 34 (4): 649–70.

Rohr, John A. 1986. *To run a constitution: The legitimacy of the administrative state.* Lawrence: University Press of Kansas.

Rommel, Jan, and Johan Christiaens. 2006. Beyond the paradigm clashes in public administration. *Administrative Theory & Praxis* 28 (4): 610–17.

Rosenberg, Alexander. 2008. *Philosophy of social science*, 3rd ed. Boulder, CO: Westview Press.

Rosenbloom, David H. 1971. *Federal service and the Constitution.* Ithaca, NY: Cornell University Press.

———. 1975. Public personnel administration and the Constitution: An emergent approach. *Public Administration Review* 35 (1): 52–59.

———. 1977. *Federal equal employment opportunity.* New York: Praeger.

———. 1978. The Burger court and the public employee. *Southern Review of Public Administration* 2 (2): 244–55.

———. 1983a. *Public administration and law: Bench v. bureau in the United States.* New York: Marcel Dekker.

———. 1983b. Public administrative theory and the separation of powers. *Public Administration Review* 43 (3): 219–27.

———. 1988a. *Public administration: Understanding management, politics and law in the public sector.* New York: Random House.

———. 1988b. The public employment relationship and the Supreme Court in the 1980s. *Review of Public Personnel Administration* 8 (2): 49–65.

Rosenbloom, David H., and Jeannette C. Featherstonhaugh. 1977. Passive and active representation in the federal service: A comparison of blacks and whites. *Social Science Quarterly* 57 (4): 873–82.

Rosenbloom, David H., and Howard E. McCurdy, eds. 2006. *Revisiting Dwight Waldo's administrative state.* Washington, DC: Georgetown University Press.

Rosenbloom, David H., and Rosemary O'Leary. 1996. *Public administration and law,* 2nd ed. New York: Taylor & Francis.

Rosenthal, Robert. 1976. *Experimenter effects in behavioral research.* New York: Irvington.

Rubin, Irene. 2007. The great unraveling: Federal budgeting, 1998–2006. *Public Administration Review* 67 (4): 608–17.

Rusaw, Carol. 2005. A proposed model of feminist public sector leadership. *Administrative Theory & Praxis* 27 (2): 385–93.

Saidel, Judith, and Karyn Loscocco. 2005. Agency leaders, gendered institutions, and representative bureaucracy. *Public Administration Review* 65 (2): 158–71.

Saloranta, Tuomo. 2001. Post-normal science and the global climate change issue. *Climatic Change* 50 (4): 395–404.

Saltzstein, Grace Hall. 1979. Representative bureaucracy and bureaucratic responsibility. *Administration and Society* 10 (4): 465–75.

———. 1983. Personnel directors and female employment representation. *Social Science Quarterly* 64 (4): 734–46.

Sandfort, Jodi R. 2000. Moving beyond discretion and outcomes: Examining public management from the front lines of the welfare system. *Journal of Public Administration Research and Theory* 10 (4): 729–56.

———. 2003. Exploring the structuration of technology within human service organizations. *Administration & Society* 34 (6): 605–31.

Sandfort, Jodi, Sally Coleman Selden, and Jessica E Sowa. 2008. Do government tools influence organizational performance? Examining their implementation in early childhood education. *American Review of Public Administration* 38 (4): 412–38.

Sardar, Ziauddin. 2000. *Thomas Kuhn and the science wars.* Cambridge: Icon Books.

Savoie, Donald E. 1994. *Thatcher, Reagan, Mulroney: In search of a new bureaucracy.* Pittsburgh: University of Pittsburgh Press.

Saxton, Gregory D., Chao Guo, and William A. Brown. 2007. New dimensions of nonprofit responsiveness: The application and promise of Internet-based technologies. *Public Performance & Management Review* 31 (2): 144–73.

Sayer, R. Andrew. 2000. *Realism and social science.* Thousand Oaks, CA: Sage.

Schachter, Hindy Lauer. 2008. Lillian Borrone: Weaving a web to revitalize port commerce in New York and New Jersey. *Public Administration Review* 68 (1): 61–67.

Schick, Allen. 1966. The road to PPB: The stages of budget reform. *Public Administration Review* 26 (4): 243–58.

Schneider, Saundra K., and William G. Jacoby. 2003. Public attitudes toward the policy responsibilities of the national and state governments: Evidence from South Carolina. *State Politics & Policy Quarterly* 3 (3): 246–69.

Schwartz-Shea, Peregrine. 2006. Judging quality: Evaluative criteria and epistemic communities. In *Interpretation and method: Empirical research methods and the interpretive turn*, ed. Dvora Yanow and Peregrine Schwartz-Shea, 89–114. Armonk, NY: M. E. Sharpe.

Schweik, Charles M., and Craig W. Thomas. 2002. Using remote sensing to evaluate environmental institutional designs: A habitat conservation planning example. *Social Science Quarterly* 83 (1): 244–62.

Selden, Sally Coleman. 1997. *The promise of representative bureaucracy: Diversity and responsiveness in a government agency*. Armonk, NY: M. E. Sharpe.

Selden, Sally Coleman, Gene Brewer, and Jeffrey Brudney. 1999. Reconciling competing values in public administration: Understanding the administrative role concept. *Administration & Society* 31 (2): 171–204.

Selden, Sally Coleman, Jessica E. Sowa, and Jodi R. Sandfort. 2006. The impact of nonprofit collaboration in early child care and education on management and program outcomes. *Public Administration Review* 66 (3): 412–25.

Shangraw, Ralph F., and Michael M. Crow. 1989. Public administration as a design science. *Public Administration Review* 49 (2): 153–58.

Shields, Patricia M. 2005. Classical pragmatism: Roots and promise for a PA feminist theory. *Administrative Theory & Praxis* 27 (2): 370–76.

———. 2006. Democracy and the social feminist ethics of Jane Adams: A vision for public administration. *Administrative Theory & Praxis* 28 (3): 418–43.

Shulman, Lee. 1986. Paradigms and research programs in the study of teaching: a contemporary perspective. In *Handbook of research on teaching*, 3rd edition, ed. M. C. Wittrock, 3–36. New York: Macmillan.

Shulock, Nancy. 1998. Legislatures: Rational systems or rational myths? *Journal of Public Administration Research and Theory* 8 (3): 299–324.

Sigelman, Lee. 1976. The curious case of women in state and local government. *Social Science Quarterly* 56 (4): 591–604.

Simon, Herbert A. 1946. *Proverbs of administration. Public Administration Review* 6 (Winter): 53–67.

———. 1947. *Administrative behavior*. New York: Macmillan.

———. 1952. "Development of theory of democratic administration": Replies and comments. *American Political Science Review* 46 (June): 494–96.

———. 1957. *Models of man*. New York: John Wiley & Sons.

———. 1969. *The sciences of the artificial*. Cambridge, MA: MIT Press.

———. 1973a. Communications: Rational and/or self-actualizing man. *Public Administration Review* 33 (5): 484–85.

———. 1973b. Organization man: Rational or self-actualizing? *Public Administration Review* 73 (4): 346–53.

———. 1995. Artificial intelligence: An empirical science. *Artificial Intelligence* 77: 95–127.

———. 1997. *Administration behavior*, 4th ed. New York: Free Press.

Simon, Herbert A., and Joseph B. Kadane. 1975. Optimal problem-solving search: All-or-none solutions. *Artificial Intelligence* 6:235–47.

Slack, James D. 1987. Affirmative action and city Managers: Attitudes toward recruitment of women. *Public Administration Review* 47 (2): 199–206.

Soss, Joe. 1999. Lessons of welfare: Policy design, political learning, and political action. *American Political Science Review* 93 (2): 363–80.

Sowa, Jessica E., Sally Coleman Selden, and Jodi Sandfort. 2004. No longer "unmeasurable"? A multi-dimensional integrated model of nonprofit organizational effectiveness. *Nonprofit and Voluntary Sector Quarterly* 33 (4): 711–28.

Spicer, Michael W. 1995. *The founders, the Constitution, and public administration: A conflict in world views.* Washington, D.C.: Georgetown University Press.

———. 2001. *Public administration and the state: A postmodern perspective.* Tuscaloosa: University of Alabama Press.

———. 2006. The legacy of David Hume for American public administration: Empiricism, skepticism, and constitutionalism. In *Handbook of organization theory and management: The philosophical approach*, 2nd edition, ed. Thomas D. Lynch and Peter L. Cruise, 261–82. New York: Taylor & Francis / CRC Press.

———. 2007. Politics and the limits of a science of governance: Some reflections on the thought of Bernard Crick. *Public Administration Review* 67 (4): 768–79.

Staines, Graham L. 2008. The relative efficacy of psychotherapy: Reassessing the methods-based paradigm. *Review of General Psychology* 12 (4): 330–43.

Stallings, Robert A., and James M. Ferris. 1988. Public administration research: Work in *PAR*, 1940–1984. *Public Administration Review* 48 (1): 580–86.

Steelman, Toddi A., and Lynn A. Maguire. 1999. Understanding participant perspectives: Q-methodology in National Forest Management. *Journal of Policy Analysis and Management* 18 (3): 361–88.

Stephenson, William. 1935a. Correlation persons instead of tests. *Character and Personality* 4 (1): 17–24.

———. 1935b. Technique of factor analysis. *Nature* 136 (3434): 297.

———. 1953. *The study of behavior: Q-technique and its methodology.* Chicago: University of Chicago Press.

Stillman, Richard J., II. 1991. *Preface to public administration: A search for themes and directions.* New York: St. Martin's Press.

———. 1999. *Preface to public administration: A search for themes and directions*, 2nd ed. Burke, VA: Chatelaine Press.

Stivers, Camilla. 1992. *Gender images in public administration: Legitimacy and the administrative state.* Newbury Park, CA: Sage.

———. 2000. *Bureau men, settlement women: Constructing public administration in the progressive era.* Lawrence: University Press of Kansas.

———. 2002. *Gender images in public administration: Legitimacy and the administrative state*, 2nd ed. Thousand Oaks, CA: Sage.

———. 2005. Dreaming the world: Feminisms in public administration. *Administrative Theory & Praxis* 27 (2): 364–69.

Swedeen, Paula. 2006. Post-normal science in practice: A Q study of the potential for sustainable forestry in Washington State, USA. *Ecological Economics* 57 (2): 190–208.

Sweeney, Kieran, and David Kernick. 2002. Clinical evaluation: constructing a new model for post-normal medicine. *Journal of Evaluation in Clinical Practice* 8 (2): 131–38.

Tashakkori, Abbas, and John W. Creswell. 2007. The new era of mixed methods. *Journal of Mixed Methods Research* 1 (1): 3–7.

Tashakkori, Abbas, and Charles Teddlie. 1998. *Mixed methodology: Combining qualitative and quantitative approaches.* Thousand Oaks, CA: Sage.

———, eds. 2003. *Handbook of mixed methods in the social and behavioral research.* Thousand Oaks, CA: Sage.

Taylor, Frederick. 1911. *Principles of scientific management.* New York: Harper & Brothers.

Taylor, Mark C. 2004. What Derrida really meant. *New York Times*, October 14.

Terry, Larry D. 2003. *Leadership of public bureaucracies: The administrator as conservator*, 2nd ed. Armonk: NY: M. E. Sharpe.

Thomas, Craig W. 1997. Public management as interagency cooperation: Testing epistemic community theory at the domestic level. *Journal of Public Administration Research and Theory* 7 (2): 221–46.

———. 2003. *Bureaucratic landscapes: Interagency cooperation and the preservation of biodiversity.* Cambridge, MA: MIT Press.

———. 2008. Symposium on qualitative research methods in political science, book review: *Social science concepts: A user's guide,* by Gary Goertz (Princeton University Press, 2006). *Journal of Politics* 70 (1): 287–89.

Thompson, Frank J. 1976. Minority groups in public bureaucracies: Are passive and active representation linked? *Administration and Society* 8 (2): 201–26.

Thompson, Fred. 1997. Book review. *Journal of Policy Analysis and Management* 16 (3): 484–89.

Thurmaier, Kurt M., and Katherine G. Willoughby. 2001. *Policy and politics in state budgeting.* Armonk, NY: M. E. Sharpe.

Torgerson, Douglas. 1986. Between knowledge and politics: Three faces of policy analysis. *Policy Sciences* 19 (1): 33–60.

Torres, Lourdes. 2004. Trajectories in public administration reforms in European continental countries. *Australian Journal of Public Administration* 63 (3): 99–112.

Turnpenny, John. 2003. *Post-normal science and the Tyndall Centre: Some critical issues.* Tyndall Briefing Note 9. Norwich, U.K.: Tyndall Centre for Climate Change Research. www.tyndall.ac.uk/publications/briefing_notes/note09.pdf.

Van der Wal, Zeger, and Leo Huberts. 2008. Value solidity in government and business: Results of an empirical study on public and private sector organizational values. *American Review of Public Administration* 38 (3): 264–85.

Van Evera, Stephen. 1997. *Guide to methods for students of political science.* Ithaca, NY: Cornell University Press.

Van Exel, Job, and Gjalt de Graaf. 2005. Q methodology: A sneak preview. www.qmethodology.net/PDF/Q-methodology%20-20A%20sneak%20preview.pdf.

Ventriss, Curtis. 1989. Toward a public philosophy of public administration: A civic perspective of the public. *Public Administration Review* 49 (2): 173–79.

———. 2000. New public management: An examination of its influence on contemporary public affairs and its impact on shaping the intellectual agenda of the field. *Administrative Theory & Praxis* 22 (3): 500–518.

Vickers, Sir Geoffrey. 1983. *The art of judgment: A study of policy making.* London: Harper & Row.

Vinzant, Janet Coble, and Lane Crothers. 1998. *Street-level leadership: Discretion & legitimacy in front-line public service.* Washington, DC: Georgetown University Press.

Waldo, Dwight. 1948. *The administrative state: A study of the political theory of American public administration.* New York: Ronald Press.

———. 1952a. Development of theory of democratic administration. *American Political Science Review* 46 (March): 81–103.

———. 1952b. "Development of theory of democratic administration": Replies and comments. *American Political Science Review* 46 (June): 500–503.

———. 1965. The administrative state revisited. *Public Administration Review* 25 (March): 5–30.

———. 1968. Scope and theory of public administration. In *Theory and practice of public administration: Scope, objectives, and methods,* ed. James C. Charlesworth, 1–26. Philadelphia: American Academy of Political and Social Science.

———. 1980. *The enterprise of public administration.* Novato, CA: Chandler and Sharp.

———. 1984. *The administrative state: A study of the political theory of American public administration,* 2nd ed. New York: Holmes & Meier.

Wamsley, Gary L. 1990. The agency perspective: Public administrators as agential leaders. In *Refounding public administration,* ed. Gary L. Wamsley, R. N. Bacher, C. T. Goodsell, P. S. Kroneberg, J. A. Rohr, C. M. Stivers, O. F. White, and J. F. Wolf., 114–62. Newbury Park, CA: Sage.

Weber, Max. 1968. *Economy and society: An outline of interpretive sociology.* London, New York: Bedmister Press.

Weber, Ron. 2004. The rhetoric of positivism versus interpretivism. 28 *MIS Quarterly,* March, iii–xii.

Weimer, David L. 1992. Political science, practitioner skill, and public management. *Public Administration Review* 52 (3): 240–45.

Weimer, Walter B., and David S. Palermo. 1973. Paradigms and normal science in psychology. *Science Studies* 3 (3): 211–44.

Weiss, Janet A. 1994. Public management research: The interdependence of problems and theory. *Journal of Public Administration Research and Theory* 13 (2): 278–85.

———. 1996. Psychology. In *The state of public management,* ed. Donald F. Kettl and H. Brinton Milward, 118–44. Baltimore: Johns Hopkins University Press.

West, William F. 1985. *Administrative rulemaking: Politics and processes.* Westport, CT: Greenwood Press.

———. 2005. Administrative rulemaking: An old and emerging literature. *Public Administration Review* 65 (6): 655–68.

White, Jay D. 1986. On the growth of knowledge in public administration. *Public Administration Review* 46 (1): 15–24.

———. 1992. Taking language seriously: Toward a narrative theory of knowledge for administrative research. *American Review of Public Administration* 22 (2): 75–88.

———. 1999. *Taking language seriously: The narrative foundations of public administration research.* Washington, DC: Georgetown University Press.

White, Jay D., and Guy B. Adams. 1994a. Making sense with diversity: The context of research, theory, and knowledge development in public administration. In *Research in public administration reflections on theory and practice,* ed. Jay D. White and Guy B. Adams, 1–24. Newbury Park, CA: Sage.

———. 1994b. *Research in public administration: Reflections on theory and practice.* Beverly Hills, CA: Sage.

White, Leonard D. 1929. *Introduction to the study of public administration.* New York: Macmillan.

———. 1955. *Introduction to the study of public administration,* 4th ed. New York: Macmillan.

Willem, Annick, and Marc Buelens. 2007. Knowledge sharing in public sector organizations: The effect of organizational characteristics on interdepartmental knowledge sharing. *Journal of Public Administration Research & Theory* 17 (4): 581–606.

Willis, Jerry. 2007. *Foundations of qualitative research: Interpretive and critical approaches.* Thousand Oaks, CA: Sage.

Willmott, Hugh. 1993. Breaking the paradigm mentality. *Organization Studies* 14 (5): 681–719.

Willoughby, Katherine G. 2004. Performance measurement and budget balancing: State government perspective. *Public Budgeting & Finance* 24 (2): 21–39.

Willoughby, W. F. 1927. *Principles of public administration.* Baltimore: Johns Hopkins University Press.

Wilson, Woodrow. 1887. The study of public administration. *Political Science Quarterly* 2 (June): 197–222.

Wise, Lois R. 1990. Social equity in civil service systems. *Public Administration Review* 50 (5): 567–75.

Wood, Curtis, and Yongmao Fan. 2008. The performance of the adapted city from the perspective of citizens. *Public Performance & Management Review* 31 (3): 407–30.

Wright, Bradley E., and Sanjay K. Pandey. 2008. Public service motivation and the assumption of person-organization fit: Testing the mediating effect of value congruence. *Administration & Society* 40 (5): 502–21.

Ya Ni, Anna, and Stuart Bretschneider. 2007. The decision to contract out: A study of contracting for e-government services in state governments. *Public Administration Review* 67 (3): 531–44.

Yang, Kaifeng, and James Melitski. 2007. Competing and complementary values in information technology strategic planning: Observations from ten states. *Public Performance & Management Review* 30 (3): 426–52.

Yang, Kaifeng, and Gerald J. Miller, eds. 2008. *Handbook of research methods in public administration*, 2nd ed. New York: Taylor & Francis.

Yang, Kaifeng, Yahong Zhang, and Marc Holzer. 2008. Dealing with multiple paradigms in public administration research. In *Handbook of research methods in public administration*, 2nd edition, ed. Kaifeng Yang and Gerald J. Miller, 25–44. New York: Taylor & Francis.

Yanow, Dvora. 1987. Toward a policy culture approach to implementation. *Policy Studies Review* 7 (1): 103–15.

———. 1999. *Conducting interpretive policy analysis*. Thousand Oaks, CA: Sage.

———. 2002. *Constructing race and ethnicity in America: Category-making in public policy and administration*. Armonk, NY: M. E. Sharpe.

———. 2003. Interpretive empirical political science: What makes this not a subfield of qualitative methods. *Qualitative Methods Section (APSA) Newsletter*, 2nd issue, Fall. http://class.csueastbay.edu/publicadmin/dyanow/qualmeth.pdf.

———. 2009. Ways of knowing: Passionate humility and reflective practice in research and management. *American Review of Public Administration* 39 (6): 579–601.

Yanow, Dvora, and Peregrine Schwartz-Shea, eds. 2006a. *Interpretation and method: Empirical research methods and the interpretive turn*. Armonk, NY: M. E. Sharpe.

———. 2006b. Introduction. In *Interpretation and method: Empirical research methods and the interpretive turn*, ed. Dvora Yanow and Peregrine Schwartz-Shea, xi–xxvii. Armonk, NY: M. E. Sharpe.

Yin, Robert K. 2009. *Case study research: Design and methods*, 4th ed. Thousand Oaks, CA: Sage.

Zifcak, Spencer F. 1994. *New managerialism: Administrative reform in Whitehall and Canberra*. Buckingham, U.K.: Open University Press.

INDEX